1,001 Ways
to Engage Employees

Help People Do Better What They Do Best

By Dr. Bob Nelson
President,
Nelson Motivation Inc.

Foreword by Dr. Marshall Goldsmith

CAREER
PRESS

This edition first published in 2018 by Career Press, an imprint of
Red Wheel/Weiser, LLC
With offices at:
65 Parker Street, Suite 7
Newburyport, MA 01950
www.redwheelweiser.com
www.careerpress.com

Material in this book has been reprinted with permission by:
Recognizing & Engaging Employees For Dummies by Dr. Bob Nelson. Copyright © 2015 by John
Wiley & Sons, Inc., Hoboken, New Jersey

The Management Bible by Bob Nelson and Peter Economy
Copyright © 2005 by Nelson Motivation, Inc. and Peter Economy, Inc. Published by John Wiley & Sons, Inc., Hoboken, New Jersey

"21 Ways to Say Thank You" from *501 Ways to Roll Out the Red Carpet for Your Customers* by
Donna Cutting © 2015 by Career Press, Inc. an imprint of Red Wheel/Weiser, Pompton Plains,
New Jersey. Used with permission of the author.

"Gracious Space" 2nd Edition by Patricia Hughes with Bill Grace © 2011 The Center for Ethical Leadership, Seattle, Washington. Used with permission of the publisher.

A Note From the Publisher
More extensive citation information for this book can be found on the author's website
www.drbobnelson.com/1001WaystoEngageEmployeesreferences

ISBN: 978-1-63265-137-2
Library of Congress Cataloging-in-Publication Data
available upon request.

Cover design by Howard Grossman
Interior photos/images by Envato Elements
Typeset in Optima and American Typewriter

Printed in Canada
MAR
10 9 8 7 6 5 4 3 2 1

Praise for *1,001 Ways to Engage Employees*

"Dr. Bob Nelson has done it again! His *1,001 Ways to Engage Employees* is a must read for anyone who manages people. In fact, it is a must read for anyone who works with people! Hundreds of effective, practical, and inexpensive ideas to engage and motivate employees told in Dr. Bob's fun and pragmatic writing style. Loved it!"

—Bob Kelleher, CEO, The Employee Engagement Group, author, *Louder Than Words* and *I-Engage*

"I've known and have respected Dr. Bob and his work for years and was especially delighted that he has focused his attention on a topic of critical importance to businesses of all types and sizes: Employee Engagement. I believe anyone who got his new book, *1,001 Ways to Engage Employees*, would benefit immensely from the practical, positive, real-life examples he shares on the researched-based factors that most impact employees to be their best at work. Get a copy for yourself and another for your manager!"

—Kevin Sheridan, *New York Times* bestselling author, *Building a Magnetic Culture* and *The Virtual Manager*

Past Praise for Dr. Bob Nelson

"Dr. Bob's books give readers ideas on how to inspire their employees to deliver the best performance every day—for little or no cost."

—Tony Hsieh, CEO of Zappos.com

"Dr. Bob Nelson provides a motherload of practical ideas and practices on building employee morale and unleashing employee potential. He represents the new frontier of organizational effectiveness—teaching us to treat our employees as we want them to treat out best customers."

—Dr. Stephen R. Covey, author, *The Seven Habits of Highly Effective People*

"Engaged employees are a vital force in any successful organization. Dr. Bob Nelson shows us how to unleash this power through a wealth of practical examples that are sure to inspire new heights of employee performance."

—J.W. Marriott, Jr., Chairman and CEO, Marriott International, Inc.

"Dr. Bob Nelson helps managers mold new management styles at their companies."

—*The New York Times*

"We all know the power of a good story. A good example provides us with much the same. Bob Nelson has given us a resource that not only shows us what others have done to get the best from employees, but what we can do as well."

—Jack Canfield, coauthor, *Chicken Soup for the Soul*

"Bob Nelson shows that there's a difference between having someone show up for work and bringing out the best thinking and initiative in each person. To do that requires treating employees more as partners, not as subordinates."

—*Seattle Post-Intelligencer*

"Bob Nelson has provided a catalogue of practical and do-able ideas and suggestions. Start anywhere in his, books but get started in enabling others to act."

—Dr. Barry Posner, Dean, Leavy School of Business, Santa Clara University

"Bob Nelson has literally rewritten the way that companies can effectively inspire people. Nelson provides tools to create real improvement in employee morale, productivity and individual, professional and personal development."

—Paul Sanders, Director, Lessons in Leadership

Other books by Bob Nelson

Recognizing & Engaging Employees for Dummies

Companies Don't Succeed, People Do! 50 Ways to Motivate Your Team

1,501 Ways to Reward Employees

365 Ways to Manage Better perpetual calendar

Ubuntu! An Inspiring Story About an African Tradition of Teamwork and Collaboration with Dr. Stephen Lundin

Managing for Dummies, 3rd Edition, with Peter Economy

Motivating Today's Employees

Keeping Up in a Down Economy: What the Best Companies Do to Get Results in Tough Times

Consulting for Dummies, 2nd Edition, with Peter Economy

1,001 Ways to Reward Employees, 2nd Edition

The Management Bible, with Peter Economy

The 1,001 Rewards & Recognition Fieldbook: The Complete Guide with Dr. Dean Spitzer

Please Don't Just Do What I Tell You—Do What Needs to Be Done!

1,001 Ways to Take Initiative at Work

1,001 Ways to Energize Employees

Empowering Employees Through Delegation

Delegation: The Power of Letting Go

Decision Point: A Business Game Book

Exploring the World of Business with Drs. Ken Blanchard, Charles Schewe, and Alex Hiam

You'll never get the best from employees by trying to build a fire under them. You've got to build a fire within them.

—Bob Nelson

CONTENTS

Who Owns Employee Engagement?

Foreword by Marshall Goldsmith

I was delighted when Bob Nelson asked me to do the Foreword for this book. We have spent much time discussing the topic of employee engagement over the years, and I was excited that he was focusing on it, first, because it is sorely needed given how little real progress most organizations have made on truly engaging their employees, and second, because I feel Bob's unique approach of identifying positive, real-life, practical strategies and examples for readers to draw from was *exactly* what could make the most difference on the topic for both individuals and organizations alike. Whereas I maintain that behavioral change is difficult, Bob consistently reminds us that change can be easier than we might think and is often simply a matter of finding the right idea at the right time to successfully implement. This book will help you do that.

One of the eternal mysteries in the field of talent management is the poor return from American companies' $10 billion investment in programs to boost employee engagement. Part of the problem is that despite the massive spending on surveying, training, and related programs, many companies end up doing things that stifle rather than promote engagement. Why is that? I believe that it's primarily because we frame the problem incorrectly, starting with who should be held responsible on the topic.

WHO OWNS EMPLOYEE ENGAGEMENT?

The standard practice in almost all organizational surveys about employee engagement is to rely on "passive questions," that is, questions that describe a static condition. "Do you have clear goals?" is an example of a passive question. It's passive because it can cause people to think of what is being done *to them* rather than what they are doing *for themselves*.

When people are asked passive questions, they almost invariably provide "environmental" answers. Thus, if an employee answers no when asked, "Do you have clear goals?" the reasons are attributed to external factors such as, "My manager can't make up his mind" or "The company changes strategy every month." The employee seldom looks within to take responsibility and say, "It's my fault." Blame is assigned elsewhere. The passive construction of "Do you have clear goals" begets a passive explanation ("My manager doesn't set clear goals").

The result is that when companies take the natural next step and ask for positive suggestions about making changes to improve things, the employees' answers once again focus exclusively on the environment, not themselves. "Managers need to be trained in goal-setting" or "Our executives need to be more effective in communicating our vision" are typical responses. The company is essentially asking, "What are *we* doing wrong?"—and the employees are more than willing to oblige with a laundry list of the company's mistakes and shortcomings.

Even if the company improves on what employees want them to do, it's too easy for employees to continue to deflect any responsibility for the behavior and subsequently tell their employers: "It's still not good enough; you've got to do more." This becomes a no-win approach to the behavior as organizations are forced to chase an ever-shifting impossible dream.

Passive questions set up individuals to shirk personal responsibility and accountability. They can give people the unearned permission to pass the buck to anyone and anything but themselves.

ALL MOTIVATION STARTS WITH THE INDIVIDUAL

How much better to start with each employee as the center of focus, so instead of asking them "Do you have clear goals?" you might ask "What are you doing to assure that your goals are clear?" or "Did you do your best to set clear goals for yourself?" Now the onus is on the employee to take responsibility to create a vision, craft a plan, and take action steps to obtain a better result.

Or take the issue of career development. If we know anything about this topic, it's that all development is self-development. That is, you can have the best skills-training programs, networking opportunities, and career paths, but if an individual isn't motivated to want to make the most of those resources and opportunities, those programs won't help that individual to learn, grow, or advance in his or her job or career.

And likewise for all the engagement categories Bob presents in this book. As you read, discuss, and apply ideas he has collected in your organization, remember to start with the individuals whose behavior you are most trying to impact. Don't just ask "What needs to be done?" but also "Who's willing to help make it happen?" and "What one or two things can everybody do to move us forward in this area?"

This approach will help assure that you're able to truly and more easily improve employee engagement with and for your employees!

—Dr. Marshall Goldsmith,
Rancho Santa Fe, California

1,001 Ways to Engage Employees

Preface

Every company today needs to obtain extraordinary results from ordinary people in order to survive, let alone thrive.

This book has a simple premise: Show people what employee engagement looks like in practice. Generally speaking, employee engagement captures the spirit, drive, and discretionary energy on the part of all its employees. It's one of those fuzzy terms in corporate America—like "employee empowerment" before it and "employee satisfaction" before that—meant to address all things, and yet, as a consequence, addresses nothing. Over the last two decades, most organizations have launched engagement initiatives or programs at their worksites. What those efforts focused on depended primarily upon how the organization measured the concept of engagement to begin with, often using the dimensions advocated by the human resources consulting firm they were working with at the time.

To help companies increase the level of employee engagement in their organization, I wanted to create a resource that started with the primary variables that most drive employee engagement, prioritize those variables in order of their greatest influence on the topic, and then identify real-life examples, techniques, and best practices of what those categories look like in practice from companies of all types and sizes. This would result in a resource that could serve as a starting point for organizations who wanted to actually move the needle in creating greater employee engagement in their organizations, not just measure the topic year after year.

After all, we already know there has been very little overall change in the number of engaged and disengaged employees over the last twenty or so years. Only three of every ten workers today is "engaged," giving full discretionary effort on his or her job today—a statistic that, according to the Gallup Organization, pretty much hasn't changed in recent decades.

About half of all employees are "disengaged" at work, that is, going through the motions but not committed to giving their best effort in their jobs, and the remainder of employees (18 percent) are "actively disengaged," even to the point of being counterproductive to the goals of the organization. Since committed employees reportedly deliver 57 percent more discretionary effort than uncommitted ones, driving greater employee engagement is critical for all organizations today. Doing it well can make the difference in driving critical aspects relevant for achieving an organization's mission and goals, its ability to attract and retain talent, and its desired financial results.

THE QUEST FOR ENGAGEMENT

Employee engagement has become the holy grail in the management of human resources. Simply stated, employee engagement is the alignment of individual and organizational goals and values to better drive both business results and personal aspirations. Ever elusive, it seems the more companies strive to attain it, the more it slips from their grasp. But the quest continues because the topic has proven to be too important to ignore.

Without an engaged staff, managers have a tough time accomplishing much—let alone the best work possible. Human resources consulting company WillisTowersWatson has noted: "Four out of every five workers are not delivering their full potential to help their organizations succeed" and the Gallup organization has estimated that disengaged employees cost the United States $450 billion annually.

In order to achieve or surpass their business objectives, companies must make sure their employees are actively engaged, inspired, and generally feel excited about their work. According to Gallup, if organizations are able to create a culture of engagement, they stand to have employees that are:

→ 480 percent more committed to helping their company succeed.

→ 250 percent more likely to recommend improvements.

→ 370 percent more likely to recommend their company as an employer.

If employees are engaged in their work, they have a greater desire to work harder, to be more productive, and to be more responsible in completing work to the best of their ability. When organizations make employee engagement a priority, they can obtain increased organizational profitability, productivity, flexibility, and employee retention, and are better able to attract talent as well. Employee engagement also creates trust between the organization and its employees so that both parties can better work together to be adaptive to changing needs and circumstances of the environment in which they operate.

This book focuses on a compilation of the primary drivers of employee engagement, prioritized in order of their impact on the topic. More importantly, it will show you what these drivers look like in practice through specific examples taken from real organizations that today are having a positive impact on these dimensions. With this book you, too, can readily learn and apply the same ideas, techniques, and best practices in your organization or work group.

Like the other 1,001 Ways books I've written before this one, I have sought to boil down the topic to the essence of what it looks like in practice through the power of real-life examples. Whether you manage just one person or are responsible for thousands, this book can help you zero in on the specific behaviors and actions that matter the most in inspiring your employees to be their best each day, every day. Best of luck in your pursuit!

—Dr. Bob Nelson
San Diego, California

FROM ENTITLEMENT TO ENGAGEMENT

INTRODUCTION

There's a big difference between getting employees to come to work and getting them to do their best work.

According to the *Harvard Business Review,* companies spend over $720 million each year on employee engagement—which is projected to rise to over $1.5 billion per year—yet, employee engagement is at a record low. Just 30 percent of employees are currently considered engaged, according to the Gallup organization—roughly the same percentage as when Gallup first started measuring the topic some twenty years ago.

What's wrong with this picture? Why is increasing employee engagement so difficult?

There's no refuting Gallup's extensive longitudinal research that systematically identified the core variables that distinguish high-performing organizations from their competitive also-rans in the marketplace. But knowing what those organizational pressure points are and actually moving the needle on those variables is apparently more difficult than anyone could have predicted.

Or are we just focusing on the wrong things and perhaps missing the forest for the trees? Are companies spending extraordinary amounts of effort (and money) to chase higher engagement scores while overlooking the fundamentals of what to do to actually impact those scores and truly engage today's employees?

Perhaps it's time to focus on the *behaviors* that truly impact employee engagement, not just the scores that measure it.

That's what this book aims to do. To show you real-life examples, techniques, and best practices of what the primary variables that most drive employee engagement look like in practice from companies that are doing those things well.

First, I found the best research framework for identifying those core employee engagement variables. Although most major human resource consulting firms have their own engagement variables they track for their clients, often a compilation of various dimensions they have found to be important, the research framework that most resonated with me and my thirty years of experience in managing and motivating employees was a statistical analysis of engagement variables conducted by HR Solutions. They examined survey data they had gathered on the topic of employee engagement from three million employee surveys and conducted a regression analysis to see which variables had the greatest impact on the topic of employee engagement.

THE ENGAGED ORGANIZATION

Following are the top ten dimensions this statistical analysis uncovered, rank ordered by the degree of significance each dimension had on influencing employee engagement. These variables are all interrelated. You can make the greatest progress on moving the needle in increasing employee engagement in your organization by focusing your efforts on these primary drivers of employee engagement as reported by employees today.

Chapter 1: Recognition

Systematically acknowledging employees and making them feel special when they do good work.

If you can only focus on one element to increase employee engagement in your group or organization, it should be recognition: making employees feel special in a timely, sincere, and specific ways when they perform well. Often called the greatest management principle in the world, recognition represents the primarily driver of employee engagement. Employee recognition is fundamental to ongoing support and motivation of any individual employee or group. The key to driving an engagement culture is to systematically recognize employees based on their performance, not just for showing up to work. While money and other forms of compensation are important to employees, what tends to motivate them to perform at their highest levels are the thoughtful, timely, personal kinds of thanks and recognition that signify true appreciate for a job well done. This chapter shares a wide range of recognition examples, techniques, and strategies currently being used by successful companies.

Chapter 2: Career Development

Helping employees learn and grow and advance in their careers.

The second most important element driving employee engagement is career development. Everyone wants to feel that where they are spending the bulk of their waking hours is leading them on a path toward something bigger and better. Along the way they want the ability to learn and apply new skills and their manager's support in doing so. In one industry-wide study, more than half of the respondents stated a strong desire for managers to support their learning of new skills in their jobs. Every employee is ultimately responsible for his or her own growth and career path. When an employee has some ambition, support from his or her manager, and options for learning and growing, they can't help but be more engaged in his or her job. In this chapter, you'll find specific examples of what companies are doing to make career development a reality for their employees.

Chapter 3: One's Immediate Manager

The actions and behaviors used by an employee's immediate manager or supervisor.

Research has shown that an employee's relationship with his/her immediate manager is the most important relationship he/she can have at work. This only makes sense because one's manager is typically the source of all work direction, coaching and guidance, and performance evaluation. Around the world, then, if you have a good boss, you have a good job—and if you have a boss that truly cares about you and your success and shows that in his/her actions, you have a *great* job! Most of us can reflect on the best managers we've had in our career and quickly list attributes and actions that most distinguished those individuals. Typically, on that list would be items such as "good listener," "took time to get to know me," "clearly communicated goals," "was approachable and supportive," "asked thoughtful questions," "made me feel important," "supported me when I made a mistake," and so forth. To be a great manager, do more of the items on this list and do them more frequently! In fact, most engagement variables are things a good manager can personally impact with their employees. In this chapter, we'll explore examples of the behaviors and actions that make for a great manager.

Chapter 4: Strategy and Mission

Linking each employee to the larger goals, vision, and mission of the organization.

Every employee wants to feel they are part of something bigger than themselves. At work this is most frequently accomplished by employees having a larger perspective about their role in the organization and their tie to the company's strategy and mission. The clearer this connection is made, the better the line of sight to the organization's vision and objectives, the more value employees will have and the more engaged they will be. Yet only 64 percent of employees feel that members of their organization understand the organization's strategy and mission. This chapter will contain examples and ideas from companies as to how they make their mission and strategies relevant to their employees on a daily basis.

Chapter 5: Job Content

The work itself: what needs to be done and how best to allow employees to do that.

Fundamental to any job is the work itself; providing clear goals, priorities, and expectations is the starting point for any job, and doing their jobs well can provide an important motivational foundation for employees. Allowing employees to have a fundamental say in how they do their work is also important, as is having challenging work. Allowing employees to fully apply themselves in getting their job done is the essence of employee engagement. This chapter will show examples of ways companies are allowing employees to do what they do best on a daily basis.

Chapter 6: Senior Management's Relationship with Employees

Having senior leadership be visible and known to employees.

Another critical dimension for employee engagement to flourish is the relationship senior management has with employees. I find the best leaders are not "above" or removed from their employees, but rather are very much involved with them, helping to lead and inspire them into the future. This chapter will show numerous examples of ways senior leaders can help drive employee engagement initiatives that are important to the organization's success that go beyond approving the budget. For example, having senior management be accessible and visible to employees is as important as playing an active role in doing things in their own jobs that consistently demonstrate their commitment to employees. This chapter will provide examples of how senior management connects with their employees in a variety of companies.

Chapter 7: Open and Effective Communication

Providing employees ready access to people and information.

All employees want to feel they are "in the know," that is, an integral part of things where they work, whether it's getting a timely answer to a question they need to complete their work; learning more about the organization's customers, products, and services; or simply knowing what's going on in other parts of the company. Managers can tap into that communication stream by being both open and transparent in sharing information as well as asking employees for their input and ideas to improve decisions, streamline processes, enhance customer satisfaction, increase revenues, and/or reduce costs. In short, involving employees in an ongoing dialogue to systematically make positive changes in the organization for both the employees, the customer, and the organization. This chapter provides many examples of open and effective communication strategies from companies that do it well that you can apply in your organization.

Chapter 8: Coworker Satisfaction and Cooperation

The quality of one's work colleagues and ease in working together with them.

Who we work with in our job is another important element that impacts employee engagement. If we like our coworkers, it's easier to come to work, spend time with them as needed, help them out, and have them help us as needed in return. If your coworkers share the same level of commitment to quality and doing good work as yourself, it further impacts how engaged you'll feel in your job—and great coworkers could even raise your standard of excellence. This chapter will provide numerous examples and strategies to increase coworker satisfaction and cooperation in your team, department, or entire organization.

Chapter 9: Availability of Resources

Having the tools, budget, and support to do the work that's expected of employees.

Having the resources to do the job one was hired to do seems like an obvious no-brainer to get the job done, let alone maximize an employee's engagement, yet we've all experienced situations in which this was easier said than done. The budget is frozen, a decision is delayed, priorities get shifted, and similar obstacles can make even the simplest plan go astray and stall or sidetrack you from your work as your focus on just getting the resources you need becomes a challenge. In this chapter, you'll learn strategies and examples from companies that have found ways to make available resources and processes a priority to those employees that depend upon those resources to get their work done in a timely, efficient manner.

Chapter 10: Organizational Culture

The shared values of the organization that shape the expectations and actions of its workers.

A backdrop in any organization for how good or bad a place it is to work is its culture: the shared norms, policies, and practices the company has established for working together, often defined by a set of core values that are publicly prioritized for all to use as guiding principles in their actions and decisions. This chapter will show examples of how organizations bring their values alive in the workplace to create work environments that both attract and retain talent on an ongoing basis.

If you have information from employees in your own organization about the most pressing engagement needs from this top-ten list, you might consider focusing on those areas first. In fact, you might consider focusing on *just* the primary or top couple of engagement needs of your employees to have the greatest chance of making improvements. I've found that when organizations try to focus on a long litany of variables, often they don't make much of any noticeable difference in their results over time because their efforts are spread too thin to truly change how things are done. Much better to truly drive a key dimension, for example, to make this year the year that recognition becomes integrated into all the organization's policies and practices and every manager's focus and behaviors.

The remainder of this book delves more deeply into each of these ten categories with numerous examples, techniques, and best practices to help show you what specific actions and behaviors gain the greatest traction in impacting employee engagement. All companies referenced in this book are featured in an index at the end of the book with their location and industry.

TREAT YOUR EMPLOYEES AS TRUSTED PARTNERS

Jon Burroughs, president and CEO of the Burroughs Healthcare Consulting Network, sums it up nicely:

Many organizations discuss engagement and alignment, which means a sense of ownership and self-interest. If you treat an employee like a commodity, they will act like one. On the other hand, if you treat an employee like an owner with a real stake in the outcome, that employee will be transformed from a subordinate into a business partner who will help your organization succeed because it is in their self-interest to do so.

Increasingly, organizations are doing just that. High-performing organizations are creating bottom-up strategies to bring the voice of line workers to senior management and often share profits with their employees as well. Delta Air Lines, which is the most profitable US commercial airline (recently earning $5.5 billion in annual profit), gave its employees over $1.5 billion in profit sharing in a recent year—adding to six consecutive years of profits shared with its employees.

In another example, health-care organizations and systems increasingly are aligning with physicians, which means giving them a piece of the enterprise in exchange for accepting accountability for clinical and business outcomes. This strategy is proving to be very successful at many of the top-performing health-care organizations throughout the country in that physicians feel a sense of ownership over their work and the work of their colleagues. This focus drives improved quality outcomes for everyone. Pride of ownership is key!

Fundamentally, you get out of human beings what you put into them. Treat them as disposable objects, and you become a disposable employer with detached, low-performing individuals. Treat them as valued, trusted partners, and you get the best of what each individual has to offer, reaping the benefits both personally and financially.

From Entitlement to Engagement

Companies today cannot afford to be stifled by a culture of entitlement in which employees do as little as possible to get by. Employees must be committed and devoted to making a difference in their organizations and must be fully engaged to do their best to excel at work.

Companies can successfully create a culture of engagement by systematically getting all of their managers to focus on those behaviors that best drive employee engagement and engage employees in those practices. To get the best of what employees have to offer the organization, managers must tap into employees' talents, interests, and skills. Getting to know employees on a personal level and asking them for their input, help, and ideas is a great starting point for any manager. In most cases, giving employees the autonomy and authority to act in the best interests of the organization and offering words of encouragement and praise along the way works wonders. Encouraging employees to pursue their ideas and supporting them in that process are also important strategies for yielding positive results in the workplace.

Managers can tap into an energy that employees themselves didn't realize existed if they are sincere in their approach and truly do have the best interests of their employees at heart. Managers must make employees feel trusted, respected, and excited about their successes and the successes of others in the organization. In return, you will get employees who are more accountable for their actions and more committed to making a difference for the organization—and themselves.

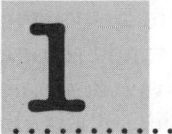

1

Recognition

There are lots of reasons why managers can't provide positive reinforcement to their employees at work, but just one reason why they must find a way:

It really works.

Recognition, thanking and praising employees for doing good work, is the number-one driver of employee engagement, significantly representing 56 percent of employees' perception of engagement where they work. This might be surprising because thanking someone is such a simple thing—almost common sense—when dealing with others. Yet, most employees report they don't get very much genuine, sincere thanks where they work. In fact, in one survey only 12 percent of employees report they receive meaningful recognition where they work, and 34 percent reported that they didn't find meaningful those things their company did to recognize them.

Yet this commonsense notion is far from common practice in most organizations today. Why is that? In my twenty-five years of working with this topic, I think it's because we often confuse the *behavior* of recognizing employees with *things* that are associated with recognition (money, gift cards, points, pins, plaques, and so on).

In fact, in my doctoral dissertation on the topic, I posed a simple question: Why do some managers use recognition while others do not? I found that a manager's access to tools, programs, or a budget for recognizing employees *was not significant* in causing them to actually recognize their employees. Translation: Employees feel special from the act of being recognized in a timely, sincere, and specific way by someone they hold in high esteem when they have done good work. This is also why many companies that spend millions of dollars on recognition tools, items, cash substitutes, and merchandise still often have a major portion of their employee population report that they don't feel valued.

According to the Aberdeen Group's employee engagement research, "By acknowledging an employee's positive behaviors and demonstrating appreciation for employee contributions, that individual worker will continue those behaviors, stay engaged with the company, and feel motivated to perform." Sixty percent of best-in-class organizations (defined as those in the top 20 percent of aggregate performers in their study) stated that employee recognition is extremely valuable in driving individual performance.

Managers and organizations struggle to systematically recognize employee performance when it happens. The notion is common sense but far from common practice in business today; managers tend to be too busy and too removed from their employees to notice when they have done good work and to thank them for it. It doesn't take much: A survey of American workers found that 63 percent of the respondents ranked "a pat on the back" as a meaningful incentive.

> On recognition: Our people want it; our people need it; and this is a cost worthy of being spent according to the feedback we get from our people.
>
> —BARRY SALZBERG, DELOITTE

The widespread lack of rewards and recognition programs at a time when it is most needed is particularly ironic because what motivates people the most tends to take so little time and money to implement. It doesn't take a huge bonus check or a trip to the Bahamas or a lavish annual awards banquet to get the best out of people. It often just takes a little time, thoughtfulness, and energy to notice what employees do, thank them for it, and encourage others to do the same. Here are some other simple forms of recognition any manager can use:

→ When you hear good news, act on it! Share it with others and thank those responsible.

→ Take a few moments at the end of the day to reflect on whose performance stands out. Write those individuals thank-you notes and leave the notes by their workstations as you leave.

→ Take time at the beginning or end of meetings to share positive news, such as letters from customers, or ask if there is any praise due from one team member to another.

→ When you read your mail, look for positive items to share with others or at staff meetings.

→ Take time to listen when employees need to talk. Be responsive to people, not just problems.

→ Make an effort to meet with employees you don't see or speak with very often. Take a break together; have coffee or an off-site lunch.

→ Remember the four-to-one rule: Every time you criticize or correct someone, plan to praise or thank that same person at least four times.

→ Take time to celebrate individual or group milestones, desired behavior, and achievements.

At the same time, some 80 percent of managers feel they are pretty good at recognizing their employees, which is a big part of the disconnect. If managers feel they're providing recognition, but employees feel they aren't receiving it, who's right? Since employee engagement stems from employee perceptions, they have the upper hand on the matter, and managers need to find ways to provide more recognition and with greater frequency.

It's not that difficult to provide more recognition, anyway. The basic behavior is quite simple. The best recognition has the following components:

→ **Soon:** Timing is important. The sooner you acknowledge someone after a success, the more that behavior or result is reinforced, and the more likely it will be repeated.

→ **Sincere:** Good recognition comes from the heart and rings true to the recipient. You can't just go through the motions if you want recognition to be valued.

→ **Specific:** Some of the sincerity in any praise comes from specifics, that is, evidence that what you're recognizing an employee for is valid and important.

→ **Personal:** Whenever possible, you should praise others directly, ideally in person.

→ **Positive:** Provide only 100 percent positive comments. Avoid the temptation to add a "yes, but" or other critique. Save that for a developmental conversation!

→ **Proactive:** Have a sense of urgency in showing gratitude to others. When you see something, say something!

Once you have established a baseline of providing employees timely, sincere, specific, positive praise and recognition, you can build upon that with other forms of recognition they value.

To successfully grow employee engagement in your organization, you must make recognition a foundational part of everyone's work life. It is critical to driving engagement and improving organization performance. In this chapter, you will find a collection of fresh examples representing the rich variety of practices others use to recognize their staff.

 Dena Saddler, an HR generalist with Infinite Electronics says, "I always do, but should not, underestimate the power of a simple 'thank you.' It should be specific about what the person did and why it was important. But mostly, it should say something about how the person's action helped you, made your day better, or made your life easier." When Saddler worked for the City of Dallas, she gave and received a lot of thank-you cards using their Thank You program. The city provided cards to every employee, who then decided to give a card to whomever they wanted—upward, downward, across, and sideways. The cards included a place to identify which of the city's values the person's action represented. "But it was mostly the handwritten, heartfelt description and why the action was so important that was most meaningful to the recipient," says Saddler. "Anyone who was lucky enough to receive one of these thank-you cards was anxious to display it in their locker or on their bulletin board, maybe to get their attention every day, maybe to remind them about why work is important, really. It's not the money; you can get that at any job."

"'Praise in public, punish in private.' I'm not sure when or where I originally heard that statement, but I live by it," says Jeff Rogers, CEO of Job Hunter Pro, a virtual company with team members from Portland, Oregon, to Atlanta, Georgia. "As a former vice president of human resources and the current CEO of a company that focuses on people, I wish more managers would embrace that simple phrase."

Joanna Adams, a supervisor for Highmark, a health insurance company in Wilmington, Delaware, writes:

I am a supervisor at my current job, and recognition is always something I have valued and held in the highest regard. I have a number of staff working under me, and I always take the time to not only acknowledge when they have excelled in some way but also to build upon their bench strengths, that is, their potential. Most employees work hard because they want to feel they matter to their employer. A hallmark of a good employer-employee relationship is not only recognizing when someone has done a good job but also for the potential they may offer. Because of that mentality, I have found my staff on the whole works harder and has a fierce loyalty to me because of that relationship. So we both end up benefiting in the long run.

Bren Anne of Bren Anne Public Relations and Marketing in Ontario, Canada, has five staff members that perform different specialties; most work remotely most of the time. She reports:

I know it sounds cliché, but we reward positive outlook with paid lunches and days off, and we offer to take on a task to help the other team member. For example, a client's needs may require a difficult resolution—maybe a client who needs a theater with a certain seating arrangement. A positive outlook remark might be, "Frustrating as it may seem, I know we'll find the perfect place for his event." When I catch positive comments, the individual gets rewarded: I do one of their tasks that day, they get a paid lunch and afternoon off, or might even get the day off, whatever my team member prefers.

Recognizing positive, on-brand behaviors within an organization is critical in keeping employees engaged. People appreciate being recognized by their supervisors, management, and peers, and it demonstrates the organization is committed to its people.

Core Creative, a Milwaukee-based advertising and branding agency with approximately fifty employees, understands that its people are its most important asset, and they developed a program for recognizing the good work of others. The Bring It! program infuses core's values and unique culture into daily activities. Employees are encouraged to nominate their peers for exemplifying on-brand behavior via an online form.

Patti Schauer, the company's vice president of finance and human resources shares

> There is no verbal vitamin more potent than praise.
>
> —FREDERICK B. Harris

specifics: "Each month, all nominees receive a token for the Bring-It-O-Matic 5000 Positive Reinforcement Machine, a refurbished gumball machine located in our lobby, which serves as a great conversation piece for clients and visitors." All nominations are also shared on the company's internal TV channel and on Yammer, their internal communication website. Nominees can win individual or all-agency prizes. Prizes include gift cards, free car washes, an office breakfast, premier parking, or their choice of an all-agency spirit day, such as Pajama Day or Dress Like Your Boss Day, college wear, Packer's NFL jerseys, and so on. The Bring It! program has proven to be a great way for team members at Core Creative to show their peers that they see their hard work and value it.

> Many managers ignore or underestimate the power of praise.
>
> —ROGER FLAX,
> PRESIDENT,
> MOTIVATIONAL SYSTEMS

"We believe what gets recognized gets repeated," says Kimberly Heller, PhD, organizational development coordinator for Iowa Specialty Hospital. "A simple but effective thing we do is to provide employee thank-you notes. Each leader writes handwritten, personal notes to employees to recognize their efforts that are in line with our organization's core values, how they demonstrate our standards of behavior. They also write notes to recognize people for going above and beyond what is expected of them. The notes are mailed to the employee's *home,* which we believe is more impactful than receiving the notes in their mailboxes at work."

Leaders use a tracking grid to see who and how often recognition has taken place. They write in the names of their direct reports (rows). The columns are labeled by the week for the month. Each week, the leaders tally when they write a thank-you note to any of their direct reports. At the end of the month when they meet with their supervisor, a senior leader, they report on the successes of their employees along with the recognition they provided.

"Another form of fun and effective recognition we do is called a gratitude exchange," adds Heller. "In celebration of Valentine's Day, each department in the hospital is assigned another department to whom they express their gratitude for contributions they make to our success as an organization. Each department uses their creativity to tailor valentine goodies to match the department and its employees."

"At the Kentucky Housing Corporation in Frankfort, Kentucky, a company with approximately 200 employees, we have a VIP program, which stands for 'valuing individuals and performance,' that provides employees the opportunity to award good work when they see," says Dr. Amy Smith, deputy executive director for business services for the agency. "The awards look like large checks made out to the employee for $75 with a detailed description of the good work that was done. Employees submit their check for payment through our normal payroll process. In the first full year of the program, 471 VIP certificates were paid to 179 employees, totaling $35,325. A total of 88 percent of employees distributed their VIP certificates and acknowledged good work of their coworkers."

> Men and women want to do a good job, a creative job, and if they are provided the proper environment, they will do so.
>
> —BILL HEWLETT, COFOUNDER, HEWLETT PACKARD

When Heather Machado was a leadership and organizational consultant at Hartford HealthCare in Connecticut, they developed a Gold Medal Manager Award based on ten leadership behaviors. It gave employees a chance to recognize their direct supervisor and explain why they deserved the award. In her role, she analyzed patterns, themes, and behaviors described in the submissions. There were then ten to twelve items submitted to senior leadership and vetted for the award. Then Gold Medal managers were selected, recognized at a system level, and recognized in their respective facilities.

When she chaired the recognition and celebration teams at Hartford Hospital in Connecticut, they created a celebration workshop that linked the core values to accomplishments of teams within the organization. Supervisors and leaders learned best practices in rewarding and recognizing their employees, and supplies were given to create celebration events/activities (balloons in branded colors, celebration templates, a budget worksheet, and so on). The result was a 10 percent increase in the organization's celebration-practices score within the organization, related to organizational and team goals.

At both locations they developed an electronic platform that linked the core values of integrity, caring, excellence, and safety, so employees at all levels of the organization can recognize each other. In doing so they were able to explain and give examples of how those they are recognizing exemplify and demonstrate the core values. Employees' supervisors also received notification of those who were recognized. In addition, all 18,000 employees went through leadership training based on their ten leadership behaviors. Those behaviors are also linked to the electronic recognition and allows for timely, specific, and meaningful recognition as employees demonstrate the behavioral expectations of the organization.

> People who feel appreciated by their employers identify with the organization and are more willing to give their best to the job.
>
> —PEGGY STUART,
> ASSISTANT EDITOR,
> PERSONNEL JOURNAL

Home Depot—the home-improvement chain based in Atlanta, Georgia—awards employees who live the company's values with Homer badges, named after the company's mascot. Employees who collect three of the badges are eligible for a cash bonus. To date, more than 400,000 Homer badges have been awarded to Home Depot employees.

Christina Zurek, solution manager with the ITA Group, an event, incentive, and recognition company, shared how their client Home Depot handles this recognition with their store associates:

Each time associates are seen demonstrating a core company value, they earn a badge that they display on their apron—part of their uniform. As a customer, it's easy to identify associates who are regularly recognized, which in turn makes it more comfortable to ask them questions. In addition, it can be a great conversation starter for a customer who may not be familiar with the program; they often ask about why there are so many badges, which then leads to an opportunity for the associate to feel recognized and share their pride in what they have achieved.

Jennifer Clark, senior vice president and director of human resources for Benchmark Community Bank in Kenbridge, Virginia, says their niche is in the small communities they serve where customers want and find a family-type atmosphere:

Our message to employees is clear: "Take care of the customer's needs." Employees do not have sales quotas—very unusual for our industry, but they know that if they take care of the customer's financial needs, the results will follow. Customers love banking at Benchmark because we make them feel special. That message is communicated from the top down.

Benchmark's values are not written down anywhere in a handbook. Employees learn about them at an onboarding class in their first three weeks with the bank. During this session, employees learn what separates Benchmark from other banks, and they learn their role in fulfilling the bank's mission to take care of the customer. To make that happen, they created the All Star Awards program.

One of their core values is caring. They created a program for peers to nominate others they see going the extra mile for customers to be All Star of the Month. Each month, the committee selects the winner from peer nominations. At the end of the year, the All Star service team selects one winner from the twelve monthly award recipients. The president presents the award and reinforces caring and going the extra mile for coworkers and customers.

Adds Clark, "Our most recent winner was a teller who had a drive-up customer mention to her that she had vision issues one day when she was cashing her check. The teller decided to contact the local Lion's Club and worked with them to get her a free pair of glasses. The woman was so grateful."

"We celebrate employment milestones during weekly meetings with foremen and laborers," says Doug Herbert, president of Herbert Construction Company in Metro Atlanta. After ninety days, new hires get a ninety-day certificate, a gift card, and a round of applause. Employees also receive certificates on the anniversaries of their start dates. They choose one of seven unknown gift cards. "Employees feel recognized for their time with the company," Herbert says. "It works for the employees we have and it is also rewarding the behavior we want repeated, which is having people staying with the company for a long time."

We are living in an age of change. If you're going to succeed in business today, you have to thrive on change, think in terms of change, assume that whatever is here today is going to be different tomorrow. You have to eat change for breakfast. The trick is to keep telling ourselves, "There must be a better way." And most of the time, there has been.

—HENRY QUADRACCI,
CEO, QUAD/GRAPHICS

CASE STUDY A: EMPLOYEE RECOGNITION

Rhett Power, a head coach in Arlington, Virginia, realized early in building his first company, Wild Creations, that they had to figure out a way to reward and recognize their employees. The challenge was they had no money. As a result, they came up with a no-budget recognition plan to ensure employees know how much they meant to the company.

We wanted to let them know every day how much we appreciated all that they were doing to make the company successful. I knew if we did that we would have lower absenteeism, better safety, decreased staff turnover, and more importantly, the team would be invested in what we were trying to achieve:

→ *Ask staff to post recognition notes to each other on a bulletin board or internal link. Add testimonies from external customers.*

→ *Give people time off. Time is the most precious gift, and people will always remember that afternoon or day to do what they love.*

→ *Send a letter to the employee's family, telling them why their loved one is so important to the company's mission.*

→ *Do one of the employee's least favorite tasks.*

→ *Give a coffee or carwash gift card, movie tickets, concert tickets. Some items can be bartered.*

→ *Allow people to work from home or present them with a flexible day certificate. You'll be amazed at what gets accomplished!*

→ Give departments their own week: Accounting Week, Programmer Week, and so on. Recognize the contributions made, take them to lunch, make certificates.

→ Create opportunities: be a mentor, chair a committee, do research.

→ Celebrate birthdays, babies, weddings, graduations, and any other happy time. Bring people together for cake and socializing. Nothing brings people together like eating a meal!

→ Establish a Wall of Fame for photos and clippings that recognize outstanding achievement. Acknowledge employees who have done exemplary work by writing up a small article about them in the company newsletter, blog, or social media.

→ Say "I'm glad you're here" and "Thank you."

"What I realized early in my business career is that recognition is more powerful than any other motivator," says Rhett.

Pretend every person you meet has a sign around his or her neck that says, "Make me feel important." If you can do that, you'll be a success not only in business but in life too.

—MARY KAY ASH,
FOUNDER, MARY KAY

CASE STUDY B:
EMPLOYEE RECOGNITION

Sherry Armstrong, owner of Award & Sign in Greenwood Village, Colorado, shares a recognition program they initiated in the last year that has drastically changed (for the good) their culture, their people, and their business.

The recognition program is a tree called Amelia, named after the word "amelioration," meaning growth or improvement. Amelia is made of vinyl, approximately eleven feet long by eight feet tall, and is located in an office area. All of Award & Sign's twelve employees have their own specific color on leaves, circles (for the center of a blossom), and starbursts (for special recognition) all explained below. Weekly, everyone has the opportunity to write on a Google Sheet their own accomplishments or those that they recognize in others. Every Monday at an all-staff meeting, they recognize those who have done something to improve the business or their workplace either through exceptional behavior or a task that would not be in their everyday routine. Their contribution might include process improvement or profit measures, among many others. They receive a leaf or a starburst in their color and a gift card worth $5 to $15, depending on the contribution.

Peer-to-peer recognition, represented by blossoms, is probably the most significant award. A circle in the employee's color is placed in the middle of the blossom. "We have found that when stakeholders receive recognition from their peers that real change occurs," says Armstrong.

There are many other symbols on the tree, each representing different accomplishments. There are twelve sparrows, one each month for the person contributing the most within that month; there are four falcons for best quarterly contributions, and one eagle for the annual superstar.

Additionally, they have special quarterly recognition. Crows are for those who receive the most kudos from customers, butterflies for those who show the most improvement, apples to those bringing a large project to fruition, owls for knowledge seekers, and squirrels for those who bring fun and happiness to the workplace. Higher-value gift cards are given for all special awards. Checks are given for the sparrows, falcons, and the eagle.

"At the base of a tree is a tiny mustard seed, which to me represents the faith that I have in the business, those whom we serve, and all the stakeholders who give so much of themselves each day to Award & Sign," beams Armstrong.

Each individual writes their accomplishment on the leaves and places the leaf or the starburst on a blossom or symbol on the tree. It is more meaningful when they pick the location and actually burnish the reward on Amelia rather than have anyone else do it.

> Once employees see that what they do makes a difference to the organization and is valued, they will perform at higher levels.
>
> —RITA NUMEROF, PRESIDENT, NUMEROF & ASSOCIATES

We are celebrating our thirtieth year in business and have had our share of ups and downs when it comes to employee performance and attitude. Since the implementation of our recognition program, it has been amazing to watch our employees look for the good in others and the things that they are doing right instead of the things that they are doing wrong. There is little to no gossip and complaining, engagement is up considerably, and the people act more as stakeholders than employees.

Amelia has meant so much to me and so drastically changed our business that I would like to share the concept with others (www.awardandsign.com). I have had several companies express an interest in having us create an Amelia for their company including, most recently, the Denver Better Business Bureau. The lessons from Amelia are vast—those we have experienced and those we have yet to experience.

At car2go's North American offices, impact is difficult since employees work in eleven different locations. The car-sharing company has worked to overcome this challenge by using a peer-recognition platform. Coworkers now show one another appreciation and stay plugged into what's happening in other offices.

Legal Monkeys, a legal-record management company based in Bryan, Texas, has an Appreciation Board—a glass picture frame—where employees can write a note and present the board to someone they appreciate. Whoever receives the board can display it on their desk until they are ready to pass it on to someone else. Each achievement is also posted on the company Facebook page to increase visibility outside of the team.

New York recruiting firm Expand Executive Search offers a peer-to-peer incentive called the Praise Pot. Every quarter, three members of the team are nominated by fellow employees to share 1 percent of the company's profits.

"Each Monday, employees at Small Girls PR firm in New York read 'high fives' calling out specific people's achievements from the week," explains associate account executive, Zoe Richards. "They're anonymously submitted from teammates, and it's an awesome opportunity to support each other and acknowledge everyone's hard work."

> We realized that our largest asset was our workforce and that our growth would come from asset appreciation.
>
> —LARRY COLIN, PRESIDENT, COLIN SERVICE SYSTEMS

Dialpad, a cloud-communications company based in San Francisco, rewards its corporate frequent-flyer miles to employees chosen by their peers for "going beyond the call of duty. To date, six employees of the 175-person staff have received all-expenses-paid trips."

When Vancouver, British Columbia, venture capital firm Growth-Works Capital wanted to improve attracting and retaining Generation Y employees, the company designed new training and rewards programs targeting these individuals. Generation Y coaching seminars for managers and a feedback program tied to rewards were two ways they implemented. Each month, managers and employees are given 1,000 points that they can award coworkers with for "a job well done." The person awarding the points must explain to the recipient why they got the award. Points can be accumulated and redeemed for various items.

> The best thing you can say to your workers is, "You are valuable; you are my most important asset."
>
> —PHYLLIS EISEN,
> SENIOR POLICY DIRECTOR,
> NATIONAL ASSOCIATION OF
> MANUFACTURERS

At MetLife Auto & Home, an insurance company located in Warwick, Rhode Island, the company's recognition program is entirely managed and administered by frontline employees—all of whom are volunteers. The program's recognition champions—the people who oversee the program in the field—are associates or local supervisors. The thirty-three winners of the company's top-tier recognition program, Best of the Best, flew to Rhode Island with their spouses, where they participated in a meeting with senior staff and were then personally honored at a dinner by the company president and top executives, and given a $1,500 travel voucher to use with their families. Since implementing this program, employee satisfaction scores in the company's claims department—MetLife Auto & Home's largest—rose from 3.89 to 4.43 on a five-point scale. Says Marge Rody, vice president of customer service operations, "Our company is stronger today than our competitors because of this program. If this remains a part of our culture, which we intend it to, it will give us an advantage over our competitors forever more."

Modeled after television's popular weight-loss reality show *The Biggest Loser*, the Coca-Cola Bottling Company of Charlotte, North Carolina, created a *Biggest Loser*-style program for the company's delivery truck drivers. The drivers were assigned to teams, and the team that lost the most collective weight received reward points that could be redeemed for merchandise, travel, and Visa gift cards. Participants—who were energized by the competition—lost an average of ten pounds each.

> With so many ways to reward people, you may ask, "How do I decide how to reward each person?" The answer is simple: Ask them.
>
> —Michael LeBoeuf, author, *The Greatest Management Principle in the World*

Instead of offering employees cookie-cutter rewards such as gift cards or plaques, Fairmont Hotels & Resorts of Toronto, Ontario, asks employees to tell the company what kinds of rewards *they* want. As a result, a cafeteria cook received a new kitchen floor, a front office supervisor received a partial payment toward a new Jeep, and a laundry attendant received a trip to London with her mother.

Through the company's Base Hits and Home Runs program, employees at holding company Burnett Companies Consolidated are able to show coworkers anywhere in the organization that they are appreciated. At the beginning of each quarter, each employee receives four base hits to give out to their coworkers as a thank-you for something they did or for doing a great job at something. When employees collect four base hits, they can turn them in for a $25 gift card for a gas station, restaurant, or department store.

Financial software maker Intuit of Mountain View, California, created an employee recognition program called Spotlight as a means for "spotlighting performance, innovation, and service dedication." The program encompasses recognition in three distinct areas:

→ Performance: for specific behavior that meets reward criteria. The majority of these monetary and nonmonetary awards can be given on the spot, providing employees with immediate recognition for exceptional behavior.

→ Innovation: for patent disclosures, patent filings, and issued patents.

→ Service: for milestone anniversaries in multiples of five years.

One unique aspect of Intuit's recognition program is that employees can have their awards converted into charitable contributions, such as the International Red Cross or an organization that provides medical services in Sudan.

The walls and machinery of a Toyota automobile manufacturing plant in India are covered with stickers marking the exact places where employees suggested innovative new ideas. The stickers—on which are written the names of the suggesters—are inexpensive but stand out to coworkers who walk by.

The engineering group of the aircraft manufacturer Boeing Company has developed an instant awards program called Pride@Boeing that emphasizes spontaneity and the personal touch. Fifty employees within the group have volunteered to serve as recognition focal points, or "focals," as they are known within Boeing. It's the focals' job to supply a steady stream of award items (valued at $10

or less) to employees to use to spontaneously recognize one another for doing something special. Typical award items handed out to employees by the department focals include such things as customized candy bars, movie tickets, calculators, and more.

Diane Symms, founder and owner of the Italian restaurant chain Lombardi's, took six top-performing employees to Italy for a sixteen-day culinary adventure. The highlight of the trip was when the group stopped in Santa Maria, a small village in the south of Italy where head chef Matthew Romeo's ancestors and relatives have lived for more than 700 years. Said Romeo, "The whole thing showed me how much Lombardi's feels about us."

Top salespeople at computer network hardware manufacturer Cisco Systems earn face time with the company's senior executives via the Chairman's Club. Limited to the company's top 1.5 percent of performers, in a recent year, winners and their spouses or partners were flown to Hawaii for a five-day stay at the Four Seasons resort on the island of Lanai. Although award winners enjoyed the typical resort amenities such as golf, tennis, spas, and the like, of greatest value was the time they spent with Cisco's senior leadership team. A series of business roundtables were arranged that brought winners together with two top-level executives to discuss business issues of interest to the sales team. According to one attendee, "One of the benefits you get from actually attending the Chairman's Club is exposure to the key execs that run the company. But secondly, career-wise, it's really beneficial. I've already noticed my profile has been raised significantly."

> It's up to you to decide how to speak to your people. Do you single out individuals for public praise and recognition? Make people who work for you feel important. If you honor and serve them, they'll honor and serve you.
>
> —MARY KAY ASH, FOUNDER, MARY KAY

Legacy Multimedia makes stars of employees to recognize their achievements. According to founder and managing partner Stefani Twyford, the company features their stars in professionally made multimedia presentations on DVD. Here are Twyford's guidelines for making an effective DVD:

→ **Get personal.** Use clips and photos of real people.

→ **Be professional.** Use professional standards to complete all production steps.

→ **Get creative.** Do something to move and entertain your audience.

→ **Add and remove.** Use editing software to add or replace people.

→ **Think history.** Archive or preserve presentations for future use.

At Recreational Equipment, better known as REI, the Washington-based outdoor gear and clothing retailer, top-achieving employees are eligible to receive the Anderson Award. Recipients are nominated by their peers and receive a variety of accolades, including a personal announcement by the vice president of their department, a Swiss Army watch, a framed certificate, and their names carved into a brick on the walkway outside the company's headquarters building. Anderson Award winners are then flown to Kent for a three-day event where they have the opportunity to meet REI's leadership team and participate in team-building events, educational seminars, and outdoor activities. Says Giselle Sampson, manager of benefits and human resources risk for REI, "One of our vice presidents or a director will take people hiking to Mt. Ranier. We've got people going sailing, we've got people going kayaking. We don't have to work too hard to get employees excited about the outdoors."

> Recognition is so easy to do and so inexpensive to distribute that there is simply no excuse for not doing it.
>
> —ROSABETH MOSS KANTER,
> PROFESSOR,
> HARVARD UNIVERSITY

At the Portugal office of New York–based global real estate firm Cushman & Wakefield, teams that complete a project go out for tapas and drinks after work, and all employees are invited to an annual three-day offsite event held at a tourist destination.

David Foos, cofounder of Teamvibe, a software start-up in San Diego, California, tells the story of one of his previous companies— Room 5, which had offices in San Diego, Silicon Valley, Sacramento, and Portland:

The year had been particularly lean on profits and we were struggling to incentivize the team. We had provided raises to top performers but had very few additional dollars to spread across everyone else. I made the decision to buy a high-end coffee machine for every office, thereby giving everyone a Christmas gift for that year. I bought four machines and each was about $3,500. The net-net was that we spent $14,000 across 100 employees. An equivalent 0.5 percent raise would have cost the company $60,000 and would have been more likely to disappoint everyone. The machines were totally over-the-top cool. We put a big red bow on every machine and hosted a "how to use it" coffee party at each location. It was a huge hit that never really lost its value; even people who weren't coffee drinkers thought it was cool. Of course, it also became the company standard for new offices as well—but that was fine by me. The machines were always a hit with candidates and new employees as well. It was a big win for the employees (and the company).

Hilcorp Energy recently gave $50,000 vouchers to each employee as part of a bonus program to double the company's size. The company also offered every eligible employee a $100,000 bonus "if the company's production rate, reserves, and value doubled by the end of the company's fiscal year, four years later." In that subsequent year, the company reached those targets, and the checks were given to employees in celebrations across every state except Hawaii.

Barbara Green, office manager for Buckingham, Doolittle & Burroughs of Canton, Ohio, explains "virtual applause":

We sent an email to our entire staff asking everyone to applaud the great efforts of our office services department at 4 p.m. at their desks. Members of that department work throughout the building, so this was a terrific way for each staff member to receive the benefit of praising at exactly the same time and in the same way.

William Pickens, owner of Pool Covers in Richmond, California, found a way to use his limited time for recognition. He often hangs a number on the wall and rewards employees who know how that number relates to the business. For example, 22.5 is the average miles per gallon of the delivery truck fleet, and those who knew that received a $10 prize.

> There is no way a workforce that is uninvolved and unrewarded will be quality conscious, efficient, or innovative.
>
> —ARRON SUGERMAN,
> *INCENTIVE MAGAZINE*

Human resource employees at Symantec Corporation give each other Serendipity Awards when someone does something worthy of recognition. At the end of each quarter, the vice president of HR randomly selects names among the recipients for prizes worth $40 to $50.

21 Days of Thank You

Here's a practical exercise from Donna Cutting, founder and CEO of Red-Carpet Learning Systems based in Asheville, North Carolina, and author of *501 Ways to Roll Out the Red Carpet for Your Customers: Easy-to-Implement Ideas to Inspire Loyalty, Get New Customers, and Leave a Lasting Impression*. She advocates providing your employees thanks for twenty-one consecutive work days to help increase your consistency in showing appreciation or as a way to reinvigorate your efforts to do so.

Day One: *Send an email thanking an employee or coworker who makes a difference in your work life. Be sincere and very specific about what they do that you appreciate. Expect nothing in return; just reach out and say thank you!*

Day Two: *Thank an employee face-to-face, telling them specifically how they make a difference to your company and/or your work day. If you work alone, pick up the phone and talk to them or leave a message.*

Day Three: *Spend some time purposefully "walking the floor" today and catch someone doing something right. When you see it, say it: Give them on-the-spot, specific praise. Try to find someone who is demonstrating one of your customer service standards and specifically share with them what they did, how it relates, and why you appreciate it. If you have time, find two or three other people and do the same for them.*

Day Four: *Plaster Positive Post-it notes! Gather a group of department heads and/or coworkers. Choose one employee you want to praise or encourage. Write positive messages on Post-it notes and plaster them all over their work area. Give someone a big visible wow and make their day.*

Day Five: *Start a chain of kindness. On a paper link, write specific words of praise about an employee or coworker. Share it with them, and let them bask in your words for a moment. Then, give them a blank chain link, and ask them to find someone else to praise and appreciate. And so on. Post the chain on the bulletin board and watch it grow as others pay it forward.*

Day Six: *Encourage an employee who needs a little lift. Let them know how they make a difference and what they do well. Ask them what they need help and guidance on and provide it. Strive to have the employee leave the conversation feeling great about themselves and their work.*

Day Seven: *Wow Patrol: Choose an employee who has really gone above and beyond. Put together a balloon bouquet and a special certificate. Gather that person's coworkers and surprise the person with the Wow Patrol. Share how they've made a difference in front of their peers, applaud together, and celebrate. Gift them with the balloons and certificate, and take a group photo.*

Day Eight: *Write a handwritten thank-you note for an employee or coworker, specifically stating how they make a difference to the team, your customers, and/or your workday.*

Day Nine: *Take a piece of paper, and with a pen or pencil, divide it into two columns. In the first column, list the names of all your direct reports. In the second column, write something positive that each person contributes to the team. Leave no one out—even if you really have to work to find the positive. Carry that list with you for a week, and as you have the opportunity, privately share the appropriate positive praise with each person on the list. Try to get through the entire list within a week.*

Day Ten: *Bring in treats to say thank you to your entire team! Bagels, pizza, cupcakes, or M&Ms (because they are marvelous and magnificent). If you'd prefer not to use food, purchase $1 lottery tickets for each staff member. Just be prepared to lose someone special should one be a winning ticket!*

Day Eleven: *Visit with a new employee or coworker. Welcome them to the organization and invite them to have lunch with you. Spend some time getting to know them and introduce them to at least three other people. Follow up with a handwritten welcome note!*

Day Twelve: *Find an employee or coworker who does a lot behind the scenes without a whole lot of recognition. Let them know that you notice their work, and specifically point out how the little things they do make a big difference.*

Day Thirteen: *Gather your team for an impromptu stand-up meeting. Ask each person to spend sixty seconds sharing good news with the team. It can be personal or professional good news. Celebrate together and go back to work! If you already have a meeting scheduled for today, begin or end it with this good news exercise.*

Day Fourteen: *Have face-to-face meetings today with at least two employees. Talk to them about their long-term goals. Where do they see themselves in five years? See where you might be able to encourage and mentor them in reaching their goals. Consider what you might be able to delegate to them that would challenge them and help them along the path to their desired future. If this is something you do regularly, choose two new people to help.*

Day Fifteen: *Regardless of what department you work in, leave a thank-you note (and maybe some treats) for the third-shift team. Be specific in your praise, and let them know how you appreciate their good work at such odd hours. If you lead people who work the third shift, show up during their shift with goodies to personally thank them.*

Day Sixteen: *Decide to give someone who has recently gone above and beyond a standing ovation! Gather ten or more coworkers to meet at a predetermined place and time. Arrange for the employee in question to come by (once everyone is assembled) and give them a long-lasting, heartfelt standing ovation! Be sure to tell them specifically what they did to warrant such a visible display of appreciation.*

Day Seventeen: *Surprise an employee with one of the following: Let them leave a half hour early with pay. Give them a long lunch and do their job for an hour. Swap one task with them—their choice.*

Day Eighteen: *Start a traveling trophy! Find something fun to use as a trophy. A big visible star-shaped necklace would be very appropriate, or a pin-on award ribbon. Give it to one of your employees and tell them specifically why they get to wear this award today. Let them know how they make a difference. The key is, they can wear it for one hour. When one hour is up, they need to find someone else who makes a difference, tell them why, and give them the ribbon or trophy to wear for an hour. Keep it going all day and see who ends up with it!*

Day Nineteen: *Write and deliver five applause certificates today. Be very specific in how each person demonstrates the standards you hold for customer experience.*

Day Twenty: *Have lunch with one or two of your direct reports. Ask for their opinions, no holds barred, about how things are going at work. What are their specific suggestions for improvement? Thank them for their input. Over the course of the next week, try to implement at least one or two of their ideas, and be sure to give them the credit.*

Day Twenty One: *Write a handwritten thank-you note to one of your employees who has really gone above and beyond lately. Instead of hand-delivering it to them, send it snail mail to their home.*

At Nucor, operating and maintenance employees and supervisors at the plant are paid weekly bonuses based on the productivity of their work group. The rate is calculated based on the capabilities of the equipment, and no bonus is paid if the equipment is not operating. In general, the production incentive bonus ranges from 80 to 150 percent of an employee's base pay.

> Our philosophy is to share success with the people who make it happen. It makes everybody think like an owner, which helps them build long-term relationships with customers and influences them to do things in an efficient way.
>
> —EMILY ERICSEN, VICE PRESIDENT OF HUMAN RESOURCES, STARBUCKS COFFEE COMPANY

Each team leader at Quicken Loans has a generous monthly budget to provide immediate, on-the-spot recognition and rewards. Top achievers are recognized at monthly meetings and dinners, and the top thirty loan officers are honored each month at a posh restaurant dinner hosted by the CEO and president. The total costs add up to more than $1 million every year.

Taj Hotels uses their special thanks and recognition system (STAR) to tie customer happiness to rewards. Employees collect points in three areas: compliments from customers, compliments from colleagues, and their own suggestions for improvement. Depending on points earned, the hotel gives employees various gift vouchers at an annual ceremony.

Judith Schmuck, head of employee engagement at online gambling giant GVD Group, teamed with Avinity for a radical new rewards solution for employee engagement. The company put employees totally in control of their social engagement platform, creating a more relaxed feel around the reward and recognition process. Everyone can earn rewards or recognize others. Schmuck says:

Our platform introduces some of the fun of playing a game into employees' lives in a way that isn't forced or fake. Choosing to take different rewardable challenges, which are linked to our values, triggers little culture-shaping shifts in outlook and behavior.

Self Regional Healthcare formed service excellence teams whose focus is to celebrate achievements, honor outstanding employees and physicians, and ensure patients receive very good care. To celebrate improvements on the Gallup survey, as well as other achievements, the company sponsored a community-wide fireworks show in February of a recent year.

RIVA Solutions, which provides services to the US federal government, has established their Kudos program to give peer-to-peer recognition. Employees, supervisors, customers, and stakeholders are invited to share their experiences with RIVA employees who went the extra mile. Each month, a name is drawn at random, and that employee receives a certificate and gift card.

LinkedIn bought 3,458 iPad Minis to thank all of its full-time employees for their hard work.

Phillips North America found a way for coworkers to acknowledge one another, with "thanks badges," up to five a week.

Employees at Royal Victoria Hospital in Barrie, Ontario, use a "fish line" for peer-to-peer recognition. The fish line is a voice mailbox to leave anonymous appreciative messages for anyone who

> Provide positive, immediate, and certain consequences for people's behaviors, and they will do what you want.
>
> —BARCY FOX,
> FORMER VICE PRESIDENT,
> MARITZ MOTIVATION

has been caught doing something right. The messages are recorded on notes and attached to a "fish" ribbon sent to the employee's manager, who then personally recognizes the individual.

> Positive reinforcement not only improves performance, it also is necessary to maintain good performance.
>
> —R.W. Reber and G. Van Gelder, *Behavioral Insights for Supervision*

Bette Gaines-Snyder, the executive director of special events at MGM Grand, sends group emails after each event that articulate people's specific contributions. Says one direct report: "When I get the emails from Bette, I feel that she is paying attention."

2

CAREER DEVELOPMENT

An often overlooked, yet primary driver of employee engagement is linking the employee to their future within the organization.

The second most significant driver of employee engagement is career development, that is, learning, development, and advancement opportunities that are provided to employees. Employees need to know that their managers are interested in their development, and managers must periodically take the time to specifically discuss and encourage employees' progress in their career, including career options and potential career paths that are available to each employee.

Managers need to support their employees in learning new skills and allow them to participate in special assignments, problem-oriented initiatives, and various other work tasks and activities. Managers should develop learning goals with each employee for the year and even for specific projects, then discuss learnings attained in the debriefing of any completed project.

Since development opportunities are a traditional motivator for most employees, as organizational needs arise, managers should ask, "Who can best learn from this opportunity?" and approach that individual. I learned this lesson early in my career when my first manager delegated an assignment to me with the words "I could do this assignment faster than you, but I thought there'd be some learnings for you in doing it."

Later I saw the same principle in practice when I worked with American Express. They developed a delegation technique they called Label and Link that they trained all their managers to use. When delegating work, managers were asked to label the task as an opportunity and link it to something that's important to the employee being considered for the assignment. To some people, this might seem like a trick of some sort, but it's the essence of employee engagement: aligning the needs of the organization with those of the employee.

Another developmental approach comes from giving employees an opportunity to experience different roles. For example, networking company 3Com believes that allowing those who work behind the scenes—especially engineers—to get out and sell to or visit customers gives them a greater appreciation for the value of the work they do. The employees in technical roles often receive customer feedback second- or third-hand and rarely, if ever, have the opportunity to sit down with a customer directly. How beneficial it is for them to engage in a dialogue that helps them do their job better and not feel as though they are operating in the dark with piecemeal information. Furthermore, when they can hear positive customer feedback first hand, it means much more.

This chapter offers a range of developmental activities and practices that organizations are currently using to maximize learning and enhance employee engagement.

"It seems to be a growing trend that employees are looking to be challenged with more amplified projects at work and rewarded with greater job responsibility," says David Kovacovich, an engagement strategist in San Francisco, California. One of David's clients, a technology company based in Silicon Valley with more than 10,000 employees implemented a known performance management strategy called SCARF, which allowed employees and managers to agree on stack ranking the employee's preferences for career development: status, certainty, autonomy, relatedness, and fairness.

Through the SCARF methodology, managers were able to better understand employee individual needs and requirements and set them on a course for development accordingly. Status-oriented employees were looking to participate in high-visibility projects, whereas certainty-oriented employees simply wanted weekly updates on their progress to goal and company progress reports.

This company found that taking performance management from one-size-fits-all to being individually structured at the employee level created a career development path that was easy for managers to help plan and follow. Promotions increased, and voluntarily leave was greatly reduced.

Software firm Full Beaker provides $1,500 per year to each employee for an educational fund to encourage them to grow professionally throughout the year. "Employees can spend the budget on books, online courses, professional conferences, coding boot camps, and so on—basically anything that makes the employee better at what he or she does for the company," says Shavkat Karimov, the company's director of SEO.

Wouldn't it be great to hire employees who are already responsible for their career development? To get a head start on maintaining an entrepreneurial spirit in your workforce, don't forget to look for partnerships with your local community colleges. For example, in the Bay Area of California, employers in eleven industry sectors rely upon the Electrical Power Systems and Instrumentation Certificate (EPSIC) program offered through the College of San Mateo. These organizations include Pacific Gas and Electric, Bay Area Rapid Transit, East Bay Municipal Utilities District, the San Francisco Public Utilities Commission, Lawrence Livermore Labs, Lockheed, Lam Research, Siemens, Chevron, and Tesla.

> Continuous learning drives everyone to find a better way, every day. It's not an expense; it's an investment in continuous renewal.
>
> —JACK WELCH, FORMER CEO, GENERAL ELECTRIC

Maureen E. White, who works in the Sacramento-based Career [Technical] Education Practices area in the California Community Colleges chancellor's office shares some exciting returns on the state's investment of $900 million. Students who participate in EPSIC boost their earnings by 81 percent, and 92 percent attain the regional living wage. EPSIC is so successful because it is one of the only programs in the state that provides hands-on training in large-scale electrical power systems. Several years ago, the college revised its forty-six-unit program to create a streamlined nineteen-unit certificate with an embedded apprenticeship. Faculty were given externship opportunities to learn the latest business needs. Curriculum was reviewed by the International Society of Automation, and the college's facilities were rebuilt from the ground up to provide state-of-the-art equipment. Students finish the apprenticeship portion of the program earning $70,000 and quickly move up a career ladder, earning $90,000 after three years.

Marketing software startup Hubspot and World Wide Tech offer their employees extensive training programs to learn and grow their careers.

Case Study:
Coaching in the Freight/ Trucking Industry

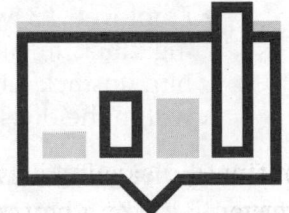

Coaching is an excellent form of focused development that companies should take greater advantage of. Dr. Terence Jackson, COO of Jackson Consulting Group, shares how he helped coach key senior-level managers for TTT Trucking, a division of CRST International Trucking, located in Warrenton, North Carolina. The company is publicly held with $275 million in annual revenues.

Dr. Jackson worked with the firm's CEO, who identified three senior-level managers for future executive leadership positions and made the commitment to provide the resources necessary to help them acquire the skills to advance. Using appropriate diagnostics, a customized one-on-one coaching process was created for each of the three individuals directly addressing their strengths and areas for improvement. Subject areas included concepts of leadership, executive leadership, strategic planning, and business development.

Each of the individuals made tremendous strides in both personal and professional development, and each has since been promoted into an executive leadership position within the company.

Results from the intervention included:

→ Employee #1 is running an entire business unit within the division. The CEO is amazed that she has been able to double revenue within eight months.

→ Employee #2 wrote her own personal and professional strategic plan with calculated ROI and proposed to the CEO the specific role she wanted to play at the firm. She subsequently was able to double revenue for the firm and had a huge impact on customer retention and growth.

> → Employee #3 was a twenty-five-year employee feeling stuck in his position. The coaching process got him unstuck, and he now runs the largest department within the division.

With the enhanced leadership stemming from this coaching intervention, the company was able to rebound from an economic downturn and are now on track to meet enhanced financial goals.

Software development services company Belatrix invests in over 120 hours of formal training per employee per year. Belatrix has one of the lowest attrition rates in the tech industry, averaging less than 12 percent, attributed in part to the attention to employee development.

Credit Karma has over 500 employees (about 80 percent of the company) enrolled in courses that run from September through November and are taught by other employees. Among the offerings are an "Intro to Coding" course for nonengineers taught by a senior engineer; "Negotiation," taught by cofounder and chief revenue officer Nichole Mustard; and a management class led by chief product officer Nikhyl Singhal. Lindsey Caplan, head of talent development at Credit Karma, says Credit Karma University is much more than a lunch-and-learn. "It also encompasses mentorship programs that help our employees develop faster here than they potentially would anywhere else."

> **We believe that most people have capabilities beyond those they are called on to demonstrate in their jobs.**
>
> **—AON HEWITT**
> STATEMENT OF PHILOSOPHY

The Boeing Company offers extensive career and leadership mentoring programs to over 150,000 employees. In one program, interns and new employees are paired with senior management who help them identify career goals and plans for various departments within the company. Diversity is the focus of the 1-to-1 Learning Program, where peers from different backgrounds meet to share perspectives and learn essential skills. The Boeing Leadership Center pairs high-potential employees with current leadership to learn interpersonal skills.

Retail giant Walmart takes career development so seriously that Walmart Academy is now one of the largest employer training programs in the United States. Faced with rebranding itself as a company focused on the needs of its employees and the needs of small towns and economically challenged cities, they have invested $2.7 billion in their training programs. They have raised wages for one million store employees. In recent years, more than 150,000 store supervisors and department managers have completed several-weeks-long training. These programs teach merchandising and motivational skills. Managers also learn how to better understand employees on a personal level.

An additional 380,000 entry-level workers have taken part in a separate training program called Pathways. Most of these workers receive a $1-per-hour raise for completing the course. Pathways offers retail math skills that employees need for stocking shelves and working cash registers. The academy, designed for experienced supervisors and managers, focuses on managing departments like a small business, such as preparing profit-and-loss statements.

One result that Walmart is especially proud of: An employee who started as a store janitor making $7.50 per hour was promoted after two years to meat department manager making $15 per hour and recommended by his former supervisor to start the assistant store manager program. This program could open opportunities for future store manager positions. Annual pay for store managers averages $170,000.

Walmart chief executive Doug McMillon predicts fewer salespeople at his stores, but says, "They'll be better paid and better trained." Results show that managers who go through the training academies have better retention rates than those who do not. Employees who report to those managers stay longer. And entry-level workers who complete a new training program are more likely to remain.

....

Walmart, Best Buy, Target, McDonald's, and Bloomingdale's closely analyze how job roles are changing and need to change to accommodate the latest consumer buying preferences. Their training programs are designed to ensure employees in new roles will be competent and committed to serving their customers.

....

At Hireology, a hiring and talent management platform, two employees were promoted a total of ten times over a four-year period. Each promotion came with new titles, responsibilities, salaries, and opportunities. This example appears to demonstrate the rule at Hireology, not the exception. The company actively encourages employees to take responsibility for developing their careers.

Joanne Denenberg, currently manager of the implementation team, who was promoted four times, says:

I started in 2014 as a sales development manager. I would basically make 100 cold calls daily to get someone on the line, hopefully, who would, hopefully, set a demo for my account executive. I did that for four months. At that point, Hireology was creating a new role for an account representative. I was asked if I wanted to do it, and I did.

> One of our responsibilities is to make sure employees are given the skills and experience to progress either inside or outside the company.
>
> —JOHN KROL,
> CEO, DuPont

Julie [Rodgers, COO] gave me great advice. She said that the way to get promoted is to do really well in the job you're doing now, ask what's next, and make life easier for the people who have the role you want. I followed her advice. I did really well in every job I had. And then I asked for something new based on the needs that I saw in the company. None of the jobs I've had here really truly existed until I helped create it.

Investopedia, an online source for financial information and education, hosts biweekly lunch-and-learns led not only by leaders but by more junior employees to encourage everyone to take leadership roles and teach others their areas of expertise.

For the past decade, Navy Federal Credit Union (NFCU) has sponsored job rotations for the organization's top management team. Each rotation lasts nine months, and successful applicants for the twenty slots are chosen on a competitive basis by Navy Federal's COO. These managers spend part of the rotation doing hands-on work in branch offices and the call center, and part of their rotation in a classroom setting. According to NFCU, these rotations of top management help the company grow its talent internally and provide participants with a real sense of accomplishment.

Computer networking subsidiary Cisco Systems GmbH, based in Hallbergmoos, Germany, enables its 3G values of grow the business, grow your team, and grow yourself by ensuring employee access to the vital 3Es: education, experience, and exposure.

Hong Kong's Trade Development Council (TDC) provides its 800 employees with more than 100 different classroom courses each year, along with an additional forty-three courses offered via its e-learning platform. One course, Staff Training and Refinement (STAR), is open to their career goals while increasing their performance and effectiveness. The course—which lasts between three days and two weeks, depending on the employee—includes training in seven broad areas, including such things as core competencies training, external seminars and conferences, functional training, and continuing education.

EVALUATE YOUR HIGH POTENTIALS

According to the Corporate Leadership Council, three attributes are necessary to evaluate high-potential employees:

→ **Ability:** The most obvious attribute. To be successful in progressively more important roles, employees must have intellectual, technical, and emotional skills (innate and learned) to handle increasingly complex challenges.

→ **Engagement:** No less important, however, is the level of personal connection and commitment the employee feels toward the firm and its mission. This attribute should not be taken for granted; just asking employees if they are satisfied with their jobs isn't enough. Instead, ask a powerful question: "What would cause you to take a job with another company tomorrow?" This prompts people to share underlying criteria for job satisfaction and say what's currently missing.

→ **Aspiration:** The desire for recognition, advancement, and future rewards—and the degree to which what an employee wants aligns with what the company wants for them—can be extremely difficult to measure. Be direct and ask pointed questions about what they aspire to and at what price: How far do you hope to rise in the company? How quickly? How much recognition would be optimal? How much money? And so on.

Shortcomings in even one of the three attributes can dramatically reduce candidates' chances for ultimate success. And the cost of mis-identifying talent can be high. You might, for instance, invest dollars and time in a star who jumps ship just as you are looking for them to take the lead on a project or problem.

AMN Healthcare has built their annual talent-assessment processes around these attributes. Each year, when they draft their succession-planning process, they interview more than 200 up-and-coming leaders. Results from the interviews allow management to gauge the level of aspiration and engagement for each employee. Then, together with each manager's assessment of an employee's abilities, the company gains a comprehensive understanding of its workforce's capabilities.

Managers at Johnson & Johnson health-care products company select high-potential individuals they believe could run a business (or a bigger business) in the next three years to participate in their development program they call LeAD. The program lasts nine months and during that time, participants receive advice and regular assessments from a series of coaches brought in from outside the company. Each participant must also develop a growth project—a new product, service, or business model—intended to create value for their individual units. Each candidate's progress is evaluated during a leadership session that is held in an emerging market such as China, India, or Brazil in order to increase participants' knowledge of the company's global operations. Graduates leave the program with a multiyear individual development plan and are periodically reviewed by a group of senior HR heads for further development and reassignment across the corporation. Johnson & Johnson managers believe that the LeAD process has accelerated individual development. More than half of the LeAD participants moved on to bigger positions in the company during the first three years after graduating from the program.

Procter & Gamble's flagship Family Care division identified a set of complex, high-impact positions that offered particularly quick development and learning opportunities for its high-potential candidates, for instance, "brand manager for a leading product" or "director of marketing for a new segment or region." Division managers dubbed these key positions "crucible roles" and began a concerted effort to fill 90 percent of those positions with high-potential employees. Candidates had to pass through three screenings to be eligible: (1) adequate qualifications to perform well in the particular crucible role, (2) stellar leadership skills, and (3) a clear developmental gap the crucible role could help them fill. Through this program, P&G has measurably increased the percentage of employees qualified for promotion: More than 80 percent of P&G's high-potential employees are ready to take on critical leadership roles each year—putting the company at a tremendous talent advantage when leadership roles need to be filled.

There's no doubt that the largest percentage of an employee's development often comes from the job they are doing, challenges they have to overcome, and new skills they have to develop. Pharmaceutical giant Eli Lilly of Indianapolis, Indiana, structures learning and development opportunities for new MBA grads accordingly: Their chairman and CEO John Lechleiter describes the recipe for the company's approach to leadership development as two-thirds coming from job experience, one-third from mentoring and coaching, and a pinch of classroom training.

Eli Lilly has found a unique way to provide its managers with the benefits of participating in different jobs while staying in their same positions. The company offers managers short-term work assignments outside their field of interest or expertise, while remaining in their current jobs. According to Lilly, managers are happy about the opportunity to expand their career skills and company knowledge without having to move to a different location or take on a long-term assignment elsewhere.

> Always assume each and every person wants to do a better job and grow.
>
> —STEVE FARRAR,
> SENIOR VICE PRESIDENT,
> WENDY'S INTERNATIONAL

At Epson, the Japanese electronics company, employees can do "executive internships" in which they spend a dedicated period of time working with company executives at different levels, learning how they spend their time, decisions they make, and so on before returning to their original position. Such a practice helps employees to see how their job relates to larger objectives in the organization.

UPS makes employee development a primary management responsibility for all its managers, who work on developing specific development plans in collaboration with each of their direct reports.

At Land's End in Dodgeville, Wisconsin, any employee requesting to work in another department are placed there for two weeks, after which they can chose to make the move permanently.

> Well-trained and dedicated employees are the only sustainable source of competitive strength.
>
> —ROBERT REICH, FORMER U.S. SECRETARY OF LABOR

At Duke Energy in Charlotte, North Carolina, professional employees of similar pay grade can swap positions with each other. These strategies make it easier to keep employees who might otherwise choose to leave the companies.

Gerard Kleisterlee, former executive vice president and co-chief operating officer of Phillips Electronics, had three priorities when he traveled: meet local management, meet a key customer, and have lunch with a high-potential manager.

A five-year study of 1,000 Sun Microsystems employees found that 25 percent of mentored employees received salary grade changes, compared to only 5 percent of the control group. Those who were mentored were found to have been promoted six times more often than others.

> We're not softhearted. It's in our interest to have an educated workforce.
>
> —GEORGE DAVID, CEO, UNITED TECHNOLOGIES

Brazil's largest cosmetics company, Natura Cosméticos of Sao Paulo, identifies promising leaders from within the organization and assigns them to shadow a high-level Natura executive for three to six months.

Rather than singling out individuals to develop as leaders, mobile telephone manufacturer Nokia Corporation of Espoo, Finland, focuses on developing teams of leaders—building their interpersonal communications and consensus decision-making skills.

To help improve the effectiveness of its leadership training efforts, General Electric Corporation of Fairfield, Connecticut, now trains entire teams of employees rather than just individuals. Chairman and former CEO Jeffrey Immelt believes this approach is having a significant impact on how much of what gets taught actually gets used on the job. Says Immelt, "At the GE I grew up in, most of my training was individually based. I could use only 60 percent of what I'd learned because I needed others—my boss, my IT guy—to help with the rest." With the change to team-based training, according to Immelt, "There's no excuse for not doing it."

Food manufacturer General Mills makes serving on a nonprofit board of directors a part of their development plans. The company believes that the service is a good way to build leadership skills among employees.

CEOs at two of America's top companies are personally involved in monitoring the development of promising employees. General Electric chairman and CEO Jeffrey Immelt keeps tabs on the development of the company's top 600 managers, while McDonald's CEO Jim Skinner regularly reviews the development of the company's top 200 managers.

Rockwell Collins, the aviation and defense company based in Cedar Rapids, Iowa, matches mentors and high performers using a web-based program.

Home-improvement chain Home Depot has implemented their Product Knowledge Recognition program to help get employees excited about learning detailed information about products carried in the company's stores. Each of Home Depot's departments, such as electrical or plumbing, has its own guide that contains more than 100 product-related questions. To be considered an expert in a particular department and receive a product-knowledge badge, employees have to correctly answer these questions. New employees are given ninety days to become an expert in their department's product knowledge, at which time they earn an increase in their base salary. After becoming an expert in their own department's offerings, Home Depot provides additional financial incentives to encourage employees to become experts in and receive product-knowledge badges for other departments.

IBM has three distinct mentoring programs: expert mentoring, career mentoring, and for new hires, socialization mentoring.

At high-end resort The Phoenician in Scottsdale, Arizona, employees are encouraged to cross-train as sommeliers, experts in wine. At last count, more than fifty Phoenician employees had passed the Court of Master Sommeliers' introductory international sommelier examination including pool attendants, an accountant, and a front desk clerk. The result is an increase in both the engagement of employees who aren't normally part of the wine team and the quantity and price of wine sold to guests of the resort. Says Sean Marron, The Phoenician's director of wine, "We've been serving a lot more great Champagne poolside—I can't keep my Cristal in stock."

> Training is everything. We believe education is the cornerstone by which we are surviving.
>
> —ANITA RODDICK, CEO, THE BODY SHOP

At Merrill Lynch Realty/Relocation Management Division of White Plains, New York, the company splits its in-house training programs into two different pieces: one for new employees and one for experienced employees. New employees are given forty hours of teaching in every part of the real estate and relocation field—all during regular working hours. Experienced employees are provided with training designed to help them move up in the organization. Aside from extensive formal classroom training, Merrill Lynch Realty/Relocation uses on-the-job training and pairs new employees up with experienced employees to accelerate the training process.

> I think as an employee, much of your professional development will focus on setting personal professional goals and putting the training provided by your company to good use. Learning more about your company's goals and objectives should also be a part of your professional development, particularly if you intend to remain with the same company and work your way up the ranks.
>
> —DEBRA DUNLAP,
> D&D INTERIOR & FASHION HOUSE

5 IDEAS FOR EMPLOYEE DEVELOPMENT

Sidney Harman, CEO of Harmon International Industries, shares his thoughts on employee development:

→ *Before they attend a course, take the time to meet with employees to discuss what you hope they will learn from it. After they attend a course, take the time to meet with employees to see what they learned and how they will apply their new knowledge.*

→ *Have employees share what they learned at a seminar or conference with the rest of the group.*

→ *Create individual development plans for each employee detailing the skills they want to learn and the development opportunities available, including potential next jobs.*

→ *Allow employees to select and attend the training course of their choice.*

→ *Encourage employees to work on an advanced degree.*

What I absolutely believe is that honoring the people who do the work can produce stunning results for the company. If the people in the factory believe there's a real effort to help improve their skills, provide opportunities for advancement, and job security, they can do things that will blow your mind.

The Yellow Pages Group of Verdun, Quebec—Canada's largest publisher of electronic and print telephone directories—subsidizes up to $2,000 of employee tuition fees for courses taken outside the company each year.

When an employee at Home State Bank in Loveland, Colorado, decided she wanted to eventually open her own jewelry store, the company's human resources manager encouraged her to view her work at the bank as a training ground for the skills she would need to someday run her own business. As a result, the employee's attitude shifted from "I'm not where I want to be" to "I'm learning the things I need to eventually succeed with my long-term dream of owning my own business." Home State Bank's openness with employee goals—both within and outside of the business—has led to higher worker morale and a turnover rate that is half the industry average.

> Education is an essential bridge between awareness and action; it provides employees with specific tools and techniques to achieve goals.
>
> —BAXTER HEALTHCARE CORPORATION QUALITY LEADERSHIP GUIDELINES

When it became apparent that it would be difficult for Red Robin Gourmet Burgers, the casual-dining restaurant chain based in Greenwood Village, Colorado, to continue to improve its already well-honed systems, senior vice president and chief knowledge officer Michael Woods decided to run a group of the company's vice presidents through Six Sigma training. None of the vice presidents worked on the operations side of the business. After the training, Woods assigned a project to test their Six Sigma skills. The project dealt with the delivery of milk shakes, which took more than four minutes to get to customers from the time they were ordered. Initially, the team consulted with the experts. One expert said the problem was the milk shake machines; the machine's capacity could not meet customer demand. Another expert said the problem was an insufficient number of spindles. The third expert felt it was a labor shortage during peak hours. The team used Six Sigma to measure all parts of the process, from the time the milk shake was ordered to the time it was delivered. Upon data analysis, the team discovered that the problem wasn't with making the milk shakes quickly, it was that no one took the milk shakes to customers after they were made. After implementing a small change to the order pickup system, Red Robin went from 32 percent on-time milk shakes to 76 percent.

The Routes of Knowledge training program for employees at automobile manufacturer Ferrari S.p.A. of Maranello, Italy, uses the themes of travel and exploration as it covers topics from computer and language skills to technical training. Specific training is linked to individual explorers: Marco Polo for worker's training, Charles Lindbergh for manager's institutional training, and Neil Armstrong for leaders' continuous training. At Campus Ferrari—a meeting that focuses on teaching Ferrari's rich history—employees participate in multimedia presentations with titles such as "Do You Know Your Company?" and "Travel Into Ferrari's History." The event ends with a dinner at which employees explore innovation and creativity. The company's Creativity Club uses employee meetings with artists, actors, chefs, and others to stimulate worker creativity and innovation.

New York financial services firm Citigroup created the Mobility Initiative to better identify and take advantage of its large pool of internal talent. The Mobility Initiative consolidated the company's eighteen different job-posting websites into one global job-posting site—making it far quicker and easier for employees to search for open jobs throughout the company. The initiative also established a set of mobility guidelines with criteria for moving to different positions and the creation of more effective career development tools.

> I think business increasingly recognizes that having a workforce that is trained, that is educated, that has the right skills is important to maintaining the great competitive steps we've made in the last few years.
>
> —STEVEN RATTNER,
> MANAGING DIRECTOR,
> LAZARD FRERES

 At Valero Energy Corporation of San Antonio, Texas—the largest independent oil refinery in the United States—promising junior employees are placed on the management fast track via the company's accelerated development program. Selected employees are assigned to mentors and specifically trained to fully assume their responsibilities when they retire or move up in the organization themselves. Coupled with an aggressive college recruitment program, Valero is able to offer young employees a clear career path to upper-management ranks—keeping them active and engaged in their jobs.

Merck, Sharp, and Dohme, the UK-based subsidiary of pharmaceutical company Merck in Whitehouse Station, New Jersey, uses their Talent Management Wheel program to develop future leaders. Through this program, the director group is given a list of ten future leaders within the organization whom they are responsible for providing with developmental opportunities.

At North Shore–Long Island Jewish Health System of Great Neck, New York, employees at every level of the organization are encouraged to expand their skills. In a recent year, the organization invested $10 million in worker training and tuition reimbursement to help facilitate the process. As a result, the organization has increased its one-year retention rate to 96 percent, patient satisfaction scores have been on the upswing, and it's not rare to encounter surgical team technicians who started out as housekeepers or secretaries.

Online-gaming company World Golf Tour pairs every employee of the company with a senior manager whose job it is to mentor the employee during the course of weekly meetings set up specifically for this purpose.

Every three months the human resources department of Home State Bank sends an email to all employees asking if they're feeling stuck in their jobs or want to acquire new job skills. Employees who respond yes to the email messages receive a personal visit from one of the bank's training or human resources specialists to review career and training options.

At FKP Architects in Houston, Texas, employees are paired with a company principal through the My Principal program. The principals help their assigned employees with career development, and they discuss salaries and prospects for promotion within the firm.

Realizing that hiring from outside can send a powerful message to junior employees about the lack of future opportunities within a company, German industrial and steel company ThyssenKrupp AG of Dusseldorf designed several rigorous processes to ensure that promising junior employees were ready to advance to opportunities of greater responsibility. To create cross-segment transparency and consistency, the company identified and clarified seven key management competencies. Subsequently, they developed a standardized appraisal process. In addition, the company created a central placement process for its top 300 managers. This process serves to promote mobility among the company's five business segments while accelerating the development of leaders throughout the organization.

> Life is sort of a buffet of learning and some things work better for others. . .so we have an array of things.
>
> —ANDREW CHERNG,
> FOUNDER AND CEO,
> PANDA EXPRESS

At Beaverbrooks the Jewellers, most managers and assistant managers have been promoted from within the organization and not recruited from outside of it.

Computer networking subsidiary Cisco Systems GmbH has created a variety of employee networks to help underrepresented groups rise up the company ranks. These networks include the Women Access Network (WAN), Cisco Black Employee Network, Gay Lesbian Bisexual Transgender Resource Group, and the Conexión network for Latino employees.

> I don't want people to sit there and passively accept leadership. I want them to become active in leadership, and that means giving them a constructive path to follow. I don't think management should be a glorified cheerleader.
>
> —JACK STACK, CEO, SRC

At Quicken Loans, employees receive 100 percent reimbursement for continuing professional education, and scholarships are available for children of employees.

Some companies take employee development to an extreme. Shipping giant Maersk sends its people overseas for three years to attend classes and learn more about the world of global shipping.

The Container Store cites its employee training programs as a major factor in retaining employees. New hires get 185 hours of training during their initial year. No other company in the industry offers as much training.

The Container Store pays based on an employee's contribution to the success of a store rather than on their position. This permits employees in nonmanagement positions to earn as much as those in management positions. Fernando Ramos was in a manager position for three years and had been promoted to it from a sales position.

But Ramos wanted to be on the floor selling, so a new position for selling and training was created for him. "I go to all the store openings to show the new people how to generate excitement on the sales floor," explains Ramos.

Executives at Razorfish noticed a troubling trend. During exit interviews, exiting employees complained that their main reason for leaving was that they didn't see good career opportunities. Dee Fischer, director of organizational development, and her colleagues conducted the company's first annual Career Month in September 2010. It provided employees with access to thought leaders, career-related learning opportunities, cross-discipline networking, and an online CareerLab portal. "We want our employees to take charge of their own careers," says Fischer.

> You can and you should shape your own future. Because if you don't, somebody else surely will.
>
> —JOEL BARKER,
> *PARADIGMS: THE BUSINESS OF DISCOVERING THE FUTURE*

Juniper Networks, a manufacturer of high-speed switching routers, was finding that they had too much voluntary attrition. In exit interviews, they learned that people were leaving because they wanted to grow their capabilities and careers. Steve Dolan, senior director of leadership and organizational effectiveness, says:

We revised our career architecture so that we have a dual career ladder: a management path and a professional path.

Juniper trains its managers to support individual ownership of their careers and creates a curriculum that teaches managers ways to develop skills that allow conversations with colleagues about their careers. Managers meet periodically with their direct reports to discuss career aspirations.

CASE STUDY: PLACING A DEVELOPMENT PHILOSOPHY INTO PRACTICE

"My favorite example that has driven my employee engagement over the past two decades is simple: Give employees the freedom to work on tasks or provide training for things they are passionate about, even if it is not totally related to their current job," says Mike Schneider, CEO of mschneiderONE in Vancouver, Canada. Mike is a business consultant with over twenty years of experience specializing in information technology strategies, customer satisfaction, user experience, leadership training, and development. He is also a stakeholder-centered executive coach certified by Dr. Marshall Goldsmith.

Here are a couple of examples of this philosophy in practice:

About ten years ago I had an employee who showed great potential, and I knew that he had skills that were desirable to other organizations that were looking for new talent. I did not want to lose this employee. I needed to find a way to keep him engaged and uninterested browsing the want ads and job sites. He was a level-1 helpdesk agent, and simply raising his salary wasn't an option at that time.

Through one-on-one discussions, I knew he was interested in programming, so I devised a plan that would benefit us both. We were going through a lean exercise at that time looking for ways to cut out the fat and eliminate repetitive tasks. I provided him with the programming tools he would need and asked him if he was interested in programming one script that would reduce the amount of time the help desk spent on tasks. He was shocked and excited that I was offering him an opportunity to break up the monotony of his day with something that he was passionate about.

Not only did he do this with great excitement, he continued to complete his day-to-day tasks. He also worked on the project in his own time (not required—his decision). He went on to create many other programs that saved the team a lot of time and the company thousands of dollars in man-hours. This employee rapidly became a senior agent, then a team lead, then a manager, and is currently a senior manager at the same company. I believe offering him the opportunity to stay engaged by assisting the team using other skills he had outside of his job description made a big difference.

Another example is an employee who wanted to take a project management course. Project management was not in their job description, but they were passionate about the concept of project management and wanted to become a project manager in the future.

I paid for this employee to take a certification course and while they were taking the course, a large North American project came up. I needed someone to represent my team and be devoted to the project. This also allowed them to practice their new skills. As it turned out this employee learned fast—likely due to their passion on the subject—and ended up representing the entire information technology department in Canada for this project. The project was a major success, and this employee also rose up the ranks at this company very quickly.

I truly believe that allowing employees to use their existing skills and/or giving them the opportunity to learn new skills that interest them, no matter how small they may seem, will benefit the employer, but more importantly, it will allow an employee to grow and become a valuable and loyal asset to that company. It will keep them interested and engaged and wanting to contribute in a positive manner.

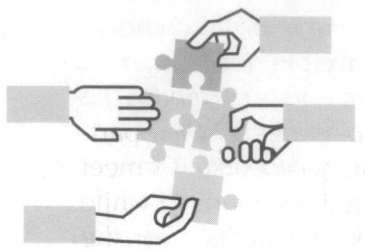

All eighty employees at Techmetals, a small metal-plating company in Dayton, Ohio, are involved in plant layout, scheduling, and delivery; rather than having just one piece of the puzzle, they work in teams.

After every team meeting, Diane Belcher, senior director of product management at Boston-based Harvard Business Publishing, asks team members to share their learnings from the meeting. More importantly, she asks them how the learnings can help further develop their roles and how they can improve client service.

Norse, a soft facilities management company, originally set up a learning program to improve literacy and numeracy among frontline workers, but its success led Norse to establish a training academy to support career development. Tricia Fuller, group HR director, says it has been important in changing the psychological contract between employees and managers, with employees reporting that they feel valued and believe they have a future with the organization.

Microsoft India tries to provide opportunities to all its employees to work across various roles, such as sales, marketing, business process outsourcing, software development, and research.

Taj Hotels established potential assessment centers to ensure career growth. The centers, along with managers, identified high performers and sent them to intensive mini-MBA programs that train them outside their area of work experience to develop them for future management positions. Taj also provides opportunities for supervisory and managerial personnel through a Career Development Committee that grooms them to prepare for higher-level positions.

After realizing that as many as 25 percent of employees quit to pursue higher education, many Indian business process outsourcing companies (companies that provide outsourced services for US companies), such as Wipro Spectramind and TransWorks formed partnerships with educational institutions and designed courses to meet the needs of the industry, allowing employees to keep working while attaining an education and providing a deeper talent pool for the companies.

Hotel management firm Winegardner & Hammons invests in its people and their long-term growth with training and internship opportunities to help them reach their professional goals. The company is also committed to promoting qualified candidates from within.

At Tata Consultancy Services, employees have the opportunity to work in multiple sectors, with different technologies, and across diverse teams in order to gain exposure to all aspects of the company. and industry. Employees are always learning and experiencing something new and developing new talents and skills, according to HR director Nupur Mallick.

A Mars employee in the Netherlands explains his company's career paths: "Mars gives everyone in the business the chance to grow. Each year, we are given the opportunity to develop our skills and prepare ourselves for our next move within Mars. Everything is possible career-wise: horizontal, vertical, cross-segment, cross-site, cross-department moves are all strongly supported by management."

> The message we give employees is that they're responsible for their career development, but we'll help them figure out which paths are the best for them to take.
>
> —ADELLE DiGiorgio,
> CORPORATE EMPLOYEE
> RELATIONS DIRECTOR, APPLE

Google has pledged $1 billion to its Grow with Google initiative that will help retrain people who may lose their jobs due to artificial intelligence. Google is sponsoring 50,000 Udacity scholarships for Android and web development, split between new and experienced developers. To help retrain 1.2 million people over a three-year period, the company has engaged Goodwill Industries.

> Ask people what they want to do. The workplace offers so many opportunities, and when we pair them with the right people, the results are amazing.
>
> —CHERYL HIGHWARDEN, CONSULTANT, ODT

Owens Healthcare offers employees the chance to shadow their coworkers for up to half a day. This program allows employees who are interested in a career change a chance to see what other positions in the company are actually like.

Employees at Let's Play Sports in San Diego have an opportunity to meet with executives every Friday to discuss MBA-level content. Executive coaching is offered to employees who meet certain qualifications, and an annual conference is offered to improve leadership abilities.

At UK-based Norse Group, any manager can request a meeting with the group HR director to request training and support for personal development. Frontline employees also have the opportunity for additional training. Norse has its own training academy, which supports career development, health and safety, and cost reduction. The results are very promising. Employees feel more valued by the company, and they see themselves having a future there.

To provide career development for their employees, LinkedIn offers a global job rotation program called [in]cubator, an idea incubator. Four times throughout the year, anyone or any team can present a product idea to executive management. The only stipulation is that the proposal must serve the needs of customers or fellow workers. Once an idea is approved, an executive mentor is assigned to the individual or team. They are allocated a maximum of three months to work exclusively on the project.

To help employees learn more about its products, Wegmans supermarkets, based in Rochester, New York, provides flexible work hours, special assignments, world travel, and college scholarships. The company is also committed to promoting from within, with two-thirds of job vacancies filled by current employees. As a result, turnover has dropped to 4 percent, compared to 100 percent for the industry overall.

According to a report issued by the Center for Creative Leadership, five key business experiences can develop employees:

✪ Challenging jobs.

✪ Other people, mostly bosses.

✪ Hardships.

✪ Coursework.

✪ Off-the-job experiences.

Employees at Whole Foods have greater control of their career path compared to employees of competitor stores. To help increase awareness of career options, the company posts all promotional opportunities and new jobs. They also encourage employees to select their teammates. Company statistics show that 90 percent of management were promoted from within.

New York–based Deloitte & Touche offers the Future Leaders Apprentice program to new hires. The program is designed to help employees plan their future and further develop essential skills they will need.

Saudi Telecom of Riyadh, Saudi Arabia, rotates 25 percent of its organization into different positions each year.

At REI, surveys revealed that skill building was very important to twentysomethings, whereas older employees wanted clear opportunities for career advancement. To satisfy the hunger for growth, REI no longer relies solely on on-the-job training, but also offers formal management training and development classes. The result has been lower turnover costs than industry averages for retail.

Each month at REI's headquarters and distribution center in Kent, Washington, the training and development team hands out copies of business-related and other books to each department. The Pass It Forward reading program makes it easy—and free—for employees to absorb ideas in classic business tomes, as well as the latest bestsellers.

Flight Centre UK, a travel agency headquartered in New Malden, United Kingdom, puts its money where its mouth is when it comes to promoting from within for its top positions, believing that doing so enhances employee engagement. Says managing director Chris Galanty, "Four of the six directors started as travel consultants in our shops. This shows people in our organization that providing opportunities is not just something we say we do—we actually live by it."

3

One's Immediate Manager

Most managers focus all their time on doing
what's urgent and have no time left to focus on
what's important—namely, their people.

Gallup found in their extensive research that the most important variable that most accounted for an employee's level of
engagement was an individual's immediate manager and all
aspects that make up that relationship between a manager and his
or her employees. This included all the things a manager did—and
did not do—in the course of managing the employee. Anyone needs
only to reflect on the best managers they've had in their career to
quickly identify the actions and behaviors that are essential for any
employee to feel supported and engaged. Do they take time to get
to know employees, allow them to ask questions, ask for their input,
listen to their concerns, and thank them for their contributions? If so,
employees are much more likely to feel trusted and respected and
valued in working for that manager—and the organization.

Taking time to personally get to know employees is essential to build strong relationships. For example, you could take a new employee out for coffee or lunch on their first day of work and ask them some questions, such as:

→ "Of all the places you could have worked, what most attracted you to work for this company? What do you hope to learn in this job?"

→ "What type of work do you like doing best? Do you prefer individual assignments or working with others as part of a team?"

→ "If a special assignment were to arise, would that be of interest to you?"

→ "Where do you hope to be in five years?"

→ "When you're not at work, what are your favorite hobbies or pastimes?"

→ "Tell me about your family. Do you have any children? Do you have any pets? What are their names?"

→ "What's your favorite food? Your favorite sport?"

And so forth. The more you know about someone, the more fodder you have to motivate that person—not to manipulate them, but to help them on their journey to be successful. Once they see through your behaviors that they are important to you, their willingness to go above and beyond to do their best on a daily basis will become real as well.

Typically, the person who is currently doing a job is in the best position to know how to do it better, so it makes sense for managers to start with those individuals as to how they can better do their jobs, supporting them as you are able. For example, if a reporting process is ineffective or costly, seek to change it or talk to the individual responsible for managing that process.

When a receptionist at Champion Solutions Group in Florida was challenged to make improvements in her work responsibilities, she suggested the expense reports she received from field sales representatives via overnight delivery reports could be sent online instead of sent overnight. The company saw a 40 percent reduction in its shipping costs. This led to company leaders seeking the advice of employees for more ways to realize cost savings.

Involving employees in decisions, especially as those decisions affect their work, is another critical manager behavior. When employees believe they have a hand in decision-making, company-wide buy-in and participation is much easier to obtain. Yet only 41 percent of surveyed employees believe the company listens to employees' ideas. Asking employees for their input shows that you respect and trust them, and will likely increase the quality of the decisions being made, even if the ultimate responsibility for decisions remains with the manager.

Support for change can't be gained without involving employees, so you need to ensure that you give employees the opportunity to be involved in decisions. Some simple ways to involve employees include:

→ Asking them for their opinions on various matters of importance to the department.

→ Inviting them to actively participate in setting objectives and revising goals for the department.

→ Establishing task forces comprising employees whose objective is to identify better ways to work.

Being flexible when dealing with employees is a hallmark of a good manager. By not being a slave to policies and instead allowing deviations as circumstances require, you will create goodwill in your relationships that you can trade on for a long time to come.

A final area of consideration for managers who want to demonstrate to their employees that they matter is how they handle mistakes. In my research, 94 percent of employees want their manager to support them when they make a mistake. This seems obvious, yet how often do we do just the opposite and find fault, publicly embarrass, and in general diminish the person who made the mistake, and in the process prove that you're the smarter of the two of you? And what does that gain you?

Bill Gates, former chairman of Microsoft, put it this way: "You can tell a lot about the long-term viability of any organization simply by looking at how they handle mistakes." How much better to take the high road and say something like "I don't think I would have done it the same way, but what did you learn from your experience? That could be the best training you'll have all year!"

Following are additional examples of how managers can make a difference in engaging their employees through their direct behaviors.

> A positive example is the best way to create the right atmosphere. There are so many things you can do to give people the security to take responsibility. Over time, you do it by measuring and rewarding performance.
>
> —JAN CARLZON,
> CEO, SAS

Tim Rogers, senior department manager for Discover Financial Services, actively promotes the idea of having a best friend at work by encouraging managers to get to know their employees. Managers attend training in two things: management skills 101 and getting to know employees individually. "Establishing a relationship with your employees comes before anything else," Rogers says.

"I cannot overstate the importance of the relationship between an employee and his or her immediate supervisor," says Robert W. Johnston Jr., clinical quality management analyst with Gateway Health in Pittsburgh, Pennsylvania.

There is a popular saying: "People don't quit companies. People quit bosses." While it is important to recognize that employees leave organizations for a variety of reasons, my experience has shown the previous statement to be undeniably true. Many managers fail to recognize that their job is not to simply ensure the completion of tasks and assignments but also to teach, coach, and nurture their subordinates. Doing so can translate into a department with better morale, greater efficiency, and more quality results. The workplace is becoming an environment where employees are in need of feeling a greater sense of purpose, fulfillment, and accomplishment. The relationship with one's immediate supervisor can make or break an employee's success in the workplace and developing those relationships benefits not only the employee, but the manager, department, and entire organization.

The *Pensacola News Journal* asked its readers to submit nominations and examples of best boss behavior. Quint Studer, founder of the Studer Community Institute, entrepreneur in residence at University of West Florida, and journalist, writes about specific examples:

→ Lindsey Cannon of Children's Home Society, who won the Best Boss Contest, takes time to get to know her employees' goals, holds them accountable for those goals, and mentors their professional development.

→ Homer and Linda Biggers of Another Broken Egg on Gregory Street do many things for staff on a personal level—from baby showers to helping get cars repaired to giving people a second chance.

→ Dave Luttrell of DAG Architects communicates difficult messages effectively, whether it be a new office initiative or constructive feedback. Most leaders can communicate what people want to hear, but it takes special talent to communicate what they need to hear.

→ Michelle Boehm of Baskerville-Donovan and her employees discuss the situation when a mistake happens. In a kind and encouraging manner, she ensures employees understand what happened and how. Then they agree on what needs to happen to prevent the same mistake from occurring again.

Handle every transaction with every person as if you will have to live with that person in a very small room for the rest of your lives.

—MICHAEL MESCON,
PRESIDENT, THE MESCON GROUP

The Boeing Leadership Center in St. Louis, Missouri, pairs current leadership with future leaders to learn the interpersonal skills they'll need to help employees reach their full potential.

Doris Lee, HR generalist for Self Regional Healthcare in Greenwood, South Carolina, shares an example about an immediate supervisor of their small team:

A team member's father passed away. The services were about an hour away, and my manager asked the majority of the team to take the hour-long drive to the team member's family home to offer condolences and deliver baked goods because they would not be able to make the services. This was truly going over and beyond to let the grieving team member know that the rest of the team cared about what she was going through.

Chuck Colmenero, the area manager at Better Business involves everyone in the branch in the annual strategic planning process so they all have a stake in the success. "Chuck has a saying," reports Roshelle Pavlin, strategic human resources consultant, 'Hire thoroughbreds and let them run!' As such, he always appreciates the skills of the professionals on his team and allows us to succeed on our own terms. He never micromanages; instead, he constantly links us to the larger picture."

Cara Silletto, president and chief retention officer for Crescendo Strategies located in Jeffersonville, Indiana, reports, "When my staff randomly mentions they love certain food, coffee shops, movies, or other things, I write those down on a secret list. When I'd like to recognize them for great work, I send them a small but meaningful token of my appreciation."

Michael Bungay Stanier, founder of Box of Crayons, says:

I recommend managers and supervisors use "the coaching book-ends" from my book, The Coaching Habit. *Start conversations by asking, "What's on your mind?" It's a better question than either "How can I help you?" (they might not need help) or "What do you need?" (they may not need anything). It's a really effective way to get quickly into the meat of the conversation: It's broader, yet also answerer-centric. Finish by asking, "What was most useful or valuable here for you?" It's a way of extracting the learning and the insight from that conversation. In our firm we've adopted "the coaching habit" for everyone, with a commitment in all our conversations to stay curious a little longer and rush to action and advice-giving a little more slowly.*

When Brian Dunn, current president and CEO of consumer electronics retailer Best Buy, completed his "rocky" first day as a Best Buy salesperson, he had a very helpful and encouraging discussion with his manager. Says Dunn, "He said, 'How did it go?' I told him it was a lousy experience." The manager proceeded to talk about the Minnesota Twins, the Minnesota Vikings, and fishing. He made it personal right away, and told Dunn to come in Saturday and he would teach him how he operated on the sales floor. "It really made a difference. What stuck with me was that the store manager was talking to me about what I was capable of doing here, and was willing to give of himself to help."

> The first responsibility of a leader is to define reality. The last is to say thank you. In between, the leader is a servant.
>
> —MAX DE PREE,
> *LEADERSHIP IS AN ART*

When managers provide performance feedback to their employees (which generally occurs on a monthly or quarterly basis), they are expected to focus on the individual and make the conversation enjoyable, perhaps even fun, instead of something to be dreaded. According to human resources director Darien Holznagel, "We focus on the individual and make it more of a fun conversation—what the individual can contribute to the organization versus what's expected. That's how we turn the corner of making it a more enjoyable process." In a recent three-year period, this approach to working with Best Buy's workforce has helped to measurably decrease employee turnover—saving the company money on training while bringing more experienced and engaged employees into customer interactions.

> Here is a simple but powerful rule: Always give people more than they expect to get.
>
> —NELSON BOSWELL

At baby bedding and accessory manufacturer CoCaLo, managers play a key role in monthly company meetings. According to founder, president, and CEO Renee Pepys Lowe, "Each leader talks about what's going on in their business. That helps keep everyone connected. What sparks interest is hearing the product stories. What retailer is interested in that product? What are the success stories? What are the stories about a mom who just sent a letter about the nursery?" As a reflection of this strategy, the company was able to maintain an average growth rate of 23 percent in a recent three-year period.

Suzie Price, managing principal at Priceless Professional Development of Marietta, Georgia, believes that managers can improve employee engagement in their organizations by cultivating four competitive leadership life skills:

1. Cultivate and share a positive belief in others.

2. Address problems quickly by focusing on behaviors and objective data; be specific and factual when talking with others about their performance.

3. Lead by inviting input and participation.

4. Listen aggressively.

Says Price about the interactions of bosses with their employees, "Value their input and provide for development and growth. Basically, it comes down to building trust."

Home improvement retailer B&Q instituted a policy requiring managers to ask employees if they had any issues they wanted addressed at morning staff meetings. Any issue raised by an employee is addressed during the course of the meeting, and managers are directed to report back to their staff the status of their issue and how it is being resolved.

Gary Olson—president and CEO of St. Luke's Hospital in Chesterfield, Missouri, which has been named one of America's 50 Best Hospitals three years in a row—believes that managers can create a workplace where employees enjoy coming to work each day by following this prescription:

→ Define your ideal workplace.

→ Start with communication

→ Maintain corporate culture.

→ Solicit feedback.

At East Boston Savings Bank, managers have adopted a "no-fault" approach to encouraging employees to report problems. Managers are encouraged to ask "probing, open-ended questions" to "get to the bottom" of employee problems, and then to thank them for raising the issue.

Managers at Henry Ford Health System in Detroit, Michigan, ensure that all employees have their email addresses and that they don't have to jump through lots of hoops to contact them with problems or opportunities. Says president and CEO Nancy Schlichting, "People appreciate and respect that privilege—I don't feel like I'm inundated with questions or issues that are not appropriate for me to deal with. Rather, it gives people an outlet if they have a concern or idea, they know they can get to me."

In a report on the impact of managers on employee engagement, research firm Melcrum Publishing found that the top ten ways for managers to build engagement among their employees are:

1. Creating a climate of open communication.

2. Helping employees understand their role in the organization's success.

3. Building trust.

4. Involving employees in decision-making.

5. Empowering employees to solve problems themselves.

6. Following through on promises and commitments.

7. Role modeling commitment to the company's goals.

8. Assisting employees in setting and reaching professional development goals.

9. Proactively soliciting feedback.

10. Recognizing exemplary behavior.

Managers at Union Bank in Los Angeles, California, are encouraged to coach their employees to become their own problem-solvers. This requires that managers have a clear picture of employees' goals and current reality. By asking questions such as "What is your goal?" and "Where are you currently in reaching your goal?" managers can better help their employees identify gaps and obstacles that prevent them from moving forward.

American Express, the New York financial services company, requires every company executive at the vice president level and above to attend a training program called Leadership Inspiring Employee Engagement. The program is designed specifically to help focus senior leaders on the skills needed to inspire employees to do their best work. In the year following implementation of the program, a survey of employees showed an increase in leader effectiveness of 3 percentage points.

The head of talent at UK-based Dyson was tasked with implementing a "martini culture," interpreted as "working any time, any place, anywhere." She developed a vision of an organization where employees were free to work where and when they were most productive. The primary challenge for the senior team was to agree to manage people as though they trusted them.

During a three-month trial, which gave people limited flexibility around core hours, their managers' role was to coach, enable, and support them to achieve their goals. The trial was a success, and all restrictions around where and when employees could work were lifted, and the dress code was removed. In the following year, voluntary turnover was reduced from 17 percent to 6 percent, and stress levels dropped significantly as people felt in control of their work-life balance.

> Employees appreciate supervisors who are empathetic to their needs. Here are five tips for establishing empathy with employees as stated in *Entrepreneur* magazine:
>
> 1. Use body language to show that you are listening.
>
> 2. Show interest with your facial expressions.
>
> 3. Affirm your understanding verbally.
>
> 4. Ask for clarification.
>
> 5. Use "we" and "us" rather than "I" and "you" whenever possible.

Burcham Hills Retirement Community decreased employee turnover by 72 percent when they implemented annual "stay" interviews with all veteran employees. The idea is to ask your team members about their current levels of engagement and how they feel about the issues of communication, growth, recognition, and trust. This initial conversation is more about understanding their current perceptions about how things are going. You don't have to get into solving the problems, which can be done later.

> You can have everything in life you want if you will just help enough other people get what they want.
>
> —ZIG ZIGLAR

A worker at REI explains why the company consistently makes lists of great places to work: "REI is a wonderful place to work. Managers pitch in and work right alongside us when it's busy. I am convinced this helps to encourage mutual respect and understanding and a sense that we're in this together."

Global science company 3M holds its leaders accountable for employee engagement by embedding engagement directly within their leadership competencies. The competency is called "develops, teaches, and engages others," and it is the foundation of annual management assessments. Managers get engagement scores from the company opinion survey.

Carolyn LaHousse, cofounder, president, and CEO of medical cost-containment and disability management company Review-Works, encourages employees to try new things, take risks, and make occasional mistakes without being punished. Says LaHousse, "Every employee is going to make a mistake—all the time. You just have to be ready for mistakes. Every time we make a mistake, there is an opportunity to do a better job." As LaHousse points out, by supporting an employee who makes a mistake, managers build the trust that is vital to building an engaged workforce.

The New Functions of Management

In *The Management Bible* my coauthor, Peter Economy, and I suggest the four traditional roles of managing, planning, organizing, leading, and controlling have now been replaced. The new functions of management that best tap into the potential of all employees are:

→ **Energize:** Today's managers are masters of making things happen. The best managers create far more energy than they consume. Successful manager create compelling visions—visions that inspire employees to bring out their very best performance—and they encourage their employees to act on those visions.

→ **Empower:** Empowering employees doesn't mean that you stop managing. Empowering employees means giving them the tools and the authority to do great work. Effective management is the leveraging of the efforts of your team to a common purpose. When you let your employees do their jobs, you unleash their creativity and commitment.

→ **Support:** Today's managers need to be coaches, counselors, and colleagues instead of watchdogs or policemen. They key to developing a supportive environment is the establishment of a climate of open communication throughout the organization. Employees must be able to express their concerns—truthfully and completely—without fear of retribution. Similarly, employees must be able to make honest mistakes and be encouraged to learn from those mistakes.

→ **Communicate:** Communication is the lifeblood of every organization. Information is power, and as the seed of business continues to accelerate, information—the right information—must be communicated to employees faster than ever before. Constant change and increasing turbulence in the business environment necessitate more communication, not less—information that helps employees better do their jobs, information on changes that can impact their jobs, and information on opportunities and needs within the organization.

Master these new functions of management, and you'll find that your employees will respond with increased engagement in their work, improved morale and loyalty, and enhanced productivity. The result is better products and services, happier customers, and a more favorable bottom line.

4

STRATEGY AND MISSION

Strategy and Mission is the North Star for any organization that should guide the focus and efforts of all its employees.

To provide a larger perspective and context for employee engagement, it's important to provide employees a clear and compelling vision of the organization as told through its strategy and mission. If employees don't know—or aren't inspired by—what the organization is trying to do, they'll find it more difficult to summon up the motivation to succeed. Frances Hesselbein, president of the Leader to Leader Institute, once put it this way: "No matter what business you're in, everyone in the organization needs to know why."

To gain clarity about the organization's mission, management guru Peter Drucker has suggested that you ask five questions to get at the core of your business. These questions help connect what your organization is trying to achieve with your customers in the marketplace:

1. What is our mission?

2. Who is our customer?

3. What does the customer value?

4. What are our results?

5. What is our plan?

Clarifying one's vision is a useful starting point for deciding what is most important for the organization—and its employees—to focus on for success. And the result needs to be a compelling purpose that can inspire everyone. "A vision is not just a picture of what could be, it is an appeal to our better selves, a call to become something more," says Harvard professor Rosabeth Moss Kanter. From that vision, you can shape your *unique competitive advantages,* that is, those aspects that you have to offer your customers that your competition does not. These advantages represent your strengths in the marketplace that you most need to capitalize on to be successful. The vision and mission then needs to be translated in ways every employee can impact.

This chapter examines examples of how companies bring the mission of the organization alive and keep it in front of employees.

Organizational leadership: First, communicate the vision and the values. Second, win support for them. Third, reinforce them.

—FREDERICK SMITH, CHAIRMAN AND CEO, FEDEX

Dolf Kahle, president of screen printer Visual Marketing Systems in Twinsberg, Ohio, believes that simple goals are the best goals. He therefore threw out the existing set of business-buzzword-laden corporate goals and replaced them with three easily understandable goals: better, faster, and cheaper.

Medical products and pharmaceutical manufacturer Johnson & Johnson provides work teams with extensive feedback on how the work they do benefits other parts of the organization. In one example, a chemical engineer in a Tylenol factory can log into a computer system that shows how his plant's output feeds into the entire division's output— and the extent to which the company is brought closer to reaching its quarterly goals. Says Tobias Kuschel, Johnson & Johnson's director of global talent management, "We believe this really creates commitment. Once you're committed, the thinking goes, you work harder and make the company more money."

Marks & Spencer, a British retailer, has each business area write its commitments on a poster, which is then displayed publicly. It helps encourage ongoing awareness and accountability.

Jeff Rogers, CEO of Job Hunter Pro, a virtual company with team members from Portland, Oregon, to Atlanta, Georgia, says:

If your mission doesn't fit on the back of a matchbook, it's probably too complex. And if your mission can't be immediately articulated by your management team, how do you expect your staff to live and breathe that mission? Clarity and focus are essential.

Our mission is to help people get and stay employed. All of our solutions have this very specific focus. An example of a key strategy that supports our mission is to bring outplacement services to the masses. To accomplish our mission, I've fostered a culture of socially responsible HR programs. We are serious about helping displaced employees get reemployed. It's a win-win for employers and employees. *Since our team is composed mostly of like-minded HR executives, the relevance of our mission is a no-brainer.*

Over the years, we've learned to mesh quality, innovation, technology, finance, and economy in ways that enable superior solutions at prices significantly below market rates. An important ingredient is the adoption of a virtual business model. We shun brick-and-mortar paradigms, the cost of which must be passed on to customers. If something doesn't directly benefit our customers, we don't do it. A downside of this philosophy is that some of my team call me cheap. I don't mind.

Keeping our mission at the forefront of team members' minds isn't difficult, in part because of its simplicity, even if they switch the words around. For example, our product development team, which includes me, hears our mission regularly as we ponder new features, benefits, and products. Likewise, our marketing, social media, and website mediums echo a common theme in support of our mission.

As a footnote regarding mission statements, close to twenty-five years ago, IBM had a mission statement that was something along the lines of "to be the world's most successful and important information technology company." That's a pretty powerful statement. It provides guidance to virtually anyone working within the company. You've gotta love the KISS (Keep it simple, stupid) principle!

> We like to think that we have an enlightened management philosophy. But enlightened management works best on enlightened employees.
>
> —HARRY QUADRACCI,
> CEO, QUAD/GRAPHICS

Bren Anne Public Relations and Marketing in Ontario, Canada, has five staff members who work remotely most of the time.

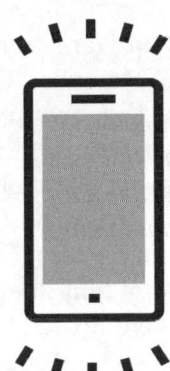

At the beginning of the month we have a group meeting, even if it's by teleconference so that we know we are all on the same page. It also allows us to address any items we were revisiting, or our mission and any strategies to achieve our goals. We have set goals, and we go over any strategies and tasks that have a timeline to complete specific client's projects, press release dates, and so on. We then sustain our connection through open communication by every method possible: Everyone has a landline, cell, email, and second contact.

Crescendo Strategies, located in Jeffersonville, Indiana, encourages staff at any level to be a part of the strategic conversation by sharing innovative ideas for growing the company, forming beneficial strategic partnerships, and creating new products. Says Cara Silletto, president and chief retention officer:

They don't have to fear "overstepping their bounds" and wait for years to contribute in a big way. Anyone can ask or share strategic questions and suggestions any time. We encourage conversations that start with "What if?" We celebrate all company successes by announcing them at staff meetings to ensure employees at all levels feel connected to the greater mission and to see firsthand how the company is impacting its clients. We mention all team members that were involved with each win, as we know the sales and consulting team delivering the results cannot do what they do without the support and operational staff keeping the organization running smoothly.

Ken Han, cofounder and senior consultant for Visionary Consulting in Shanghai, China, says, "Participation is the gateway for enhancing engagement either vertically or horizontally. Employees or coworkers will be significantly more engaged if they're invited to cocreate the goals, strategies, and plans they are a part of executing."

For a horizontal example, a director of a supply chain invited their internal customers and stakeholders to the discussion of determining the group's goals, approaches, and priorities. Those who were invited shared with the team their concerns, worries, expectations, and suggestions. This process made the execution of the plans discussed much smoother in the future since key stakeholders and customers were engaged throughout. For a vertical integration example, a functional leader brings all his direct reports together with representatives at various levels of management as well as frontline workers.

"To increase employee participation, you have to have a culture and mechanism that encourages participation, and the opportunities have to be created and announced and then facilitated," says Han. "This requires leaders at each level to be able to be facilitators and coaches." For example, a manager sets rules for participating in his planning and goal-setting process at his level. All his team members are invited to post their comments on his plans under the headings of "Change," "Concerns," and "Ideas." During the goal-setting season, he invites them to do an environmental analysis upon which his goals and plan will be based. Later, he asks them to attend a series of problem-solving and planning workshops. And lastly, to attend a plenary session for consolidating confidence, commitment, and alignment. As Han reports:

We've found that more and more clients have abandoned KPI (key performance indicators) as their major performance management tool for achieving an organization's mission and objectives and have started to embrace OKR (objectives and key results) instead. Some smart managers find success with a more behavioral approach, that is, focusing employees on "the three most important things to do weekly" method for managing the focus of each team member, which is much easier than using KPI.

Other employee engagement strategies that we've found to be effective:

→ *Mentoring as a format of partnership is amazing and very effective in engaging employees.*

→ *Having sports teams in the organization helps to build a basic layer of the culture that encourages everyone to be more competitive. (Companies that have sports teams are more engaged and resilient.)*

→ *You can also find and develop highly engaged employees called "transformers," then form coalition teams around them, which also greatly helps to enhance employee engagement throughout the organization.*

Tracie Sponenberg, senior vice president of human resources at The Granite Group, based in Concord, New Hampshire reports:

Each quarter, every quarter, our CEO, COO, and chairman visit every one of our thirty-four locations for a quarterly meeting. These meetings are focused on financial metrics and strategy. Every one of our team members, from truck drivers to managers, attends and is updated on company performance, branch performance, and progress with our strategy. You can ask any of our employees what the main strategic focus of our company is—and they will know. Our locations also share daily sales information with their team, so everyone knows how the location is performing, and can understand their impact on their location and the organization.

David Kovacovich, an engagement strategist in San Francisco, California, shares how one of his clients, a technology company based in Silicon Valley with more than 10,000 employees, was struggling to streamline their innovation strategy.

Projects were failing, old thinking wasn't competing, and the competition was catching up in the marketplace. This company looked to their newer hires to amplify their innovation strategy, asking them "What are we missing? What are you seeing?" They issued a challenge to all employees to submit ideas for new product development, service models, or internal dynamic building. Employees were called upon to issue their ideas in just three slides.

Over 300 new ideas were submitted, and a committee was assigned to evaluate the ideas, holding preliminary calls with those that submitted the best ideas. The top five ideators were called upon to present in *Shark Tank* style at the annual international company meeting. The company rewarded everyone by adopting their ideas, and they were assigned as project leads to bring the ideas to market.

To inculcate their corporate values, RB, a 180-employee IT company servicing the financial sector in Iceland, decided to tap into the

high interest employees have in music, reports Herdis Pala, a corporate trainer and business consultant for Pafugl ehf/Peacock. Employees at RB participate in ten bands and choirs at the company. They asked employees to find Icelandic songs and lyrics to show the meaning of the company's values: professionalism (an old Icelandic fisherman's song), safety (a fairly new heavy metal song), and passion (a love song from the late 1990s). They subsequently decorated their office walls with lyrics that represent the meaning of their corporate values.

"Employees have a visual of our firm's values in sight all day, which keeps them top of mind and brings smiles to the faces of their guests and customers," says Herdis.

Michele Moore, founder and CEO of Southwest Human Capital, based in Albuquerque, New Mexico, recalls working with Quad Learning, a company focused on fostering opportunities for international students to attend their "dream" colleges.

> To any organizational problem first ask, "What is the best solution?" Then ask, "What can be done?"
>
> —PETER DRUCKER, MANAGEMENT CONSULTANT

We created a monthly newsletter that featured a "Values in Action" segment. Employees were asked to give examples when they witnessed colleagues demonstrating our core values and principles. They loved it. The illustrations used—such as when employees clearly went above and beyond to satisfy a client or suggest something innovative—clearly encouraged and inspired everyone. In addition to serving as recognition, this reinforced our values over and over, and made them part of our firm's everyday vernacular.

Acceleration Partners, a Boston-based marketing firm reviewed its vision and created "Vivid Vision," a new document highlighting values, goals, and how employees fit in. The firm asked employees to contribute and help shape the document.

Zuora, an order-to-cash platform in San Mateo, California, started a pilot appreciation program that linked core company values to its recognition practices.

Case Study: Linking Strategy via Recognition

A market research team in a *Fortune* 500 high-technology company had a strategy to help the company grow. Their challenge: "How can we motivate individuals to adapt the behaviors that most effectively tie to this strategy?" Along with other initiatives, the team's executive leadership implemented a recognition program to link individuals to the company's strategies.

Four key attributes were identified as critical to the success of team members helping the company grow, and these were incorporated into the recognition program:

1. **Integration:** Recognized individuals and teams who proactively built a shared agenda with business leaders and collaborated across teams to deliver meaningful business outcomes.

2. **Innovation:** Recognized individuals and teams who demonstrated thought leadership, applied unique expertise by building new capabilities, and delivered innovative solutions to solve a critical business issue.

3. **Technical expertise:** Recognized individuals who were technical exemplars and thought leaders in their respective disciplines.

4. **Leadership:** Recognized managers and team leads who championed action with business leaders to achieve meaningful outcomes.

Organization development managed the process of disseminating information about the program, collecting nominations, and preparing the leadership team so they could make their selections. A worldwide virtual team event was held twice a year to announce the winners and recognize the projects, behaviors, and outcomes that mattered most and linked best to the team strategy. Follow-up activities included winners presenting their projects and providing counsel to a wide range of people across the company.

The recognition program was deemed very successful. Individuals across the team were more motivated to integrate, innovate, lead, and develop the technical expertise required to help the company grow. Other teams at the company leveraged the recognition program to tie team behavior to their strategies. And interestingly, there were no monetary awards associated with this program. The visibility and recognition of an individual's work across the organization and with their peers were strong enough motivators on their own.

This global program was internally run. Specifically, a member of the OD team was responsible for the recognition program and handled all processes. In addition to dissemination, collection, and preparation, they also handled all communications. The formal program was conducted twice a year for several years so it became institutionalized. It was systematic, not ad hoc, with no external help.

Vision is long term, and should not change every two to three years, but it should be evaluated and measured. That is done by communication.

—JAMES SPEED,
PRESIDENT AND CEO,
NORTH CAROLINA MUTUAL LIFE INSURANCE

Dr. Amy Smith, deputy executive director for business services at the Kentucky Housing Corporation in Frankfort, Kentucky, says:

Prior to the start of each fiscal year in July, the executive team in consultation with the directors and managers set corporate strategic direction. This consists of three to five concise and easily explained strategies. We provide a laminated copy of these strategies to share with each employee.

Additionally, every department creates a business plan and a scorecard to support the corporate strategies. For employees, the strategies are used in our in-house created employee performance evaluation system. So, each performance goal for the staff links to a departmental goal and corporate strategy.

Actions toward achieving the strategies are discussed at the management level at least quarterly, and in departments on a monthly or similar routine basis. Also, all items are placed on a corporate calendar to visually see where areas may be falling behind. We pride ourselves that most staff can share corporate strategies and speak about how strategy impacts their daily work. In a recent board meeting, we adopted new technology allowing board members to access all  *board documents with a tablet instead of in a large paper binder. Line-level technology services team members attended the meeting to give support to the new users. When asked, the staff let board members know that their new technology was a part of achieving corporate strategy number four: Support flexible, mobile, collaborative, and remote work.*

To ensure employees connect with the company's vision and mission, the CEO of Farm Bureau Financial Services in Des Moines, Iowa, called upon his leaders to brainstorm supportive ideas. One result: All computer screens were changed to show a list of company values.

To help employees see how their job efforts come to fruition, founder Elon Musk of SpaceX gathers everyone around mission control to experience rocket launches. To inspire them further, he treats them to private screenings of space-related movies such as *Gravity* and *The Martian*.

Several companies today have added a new position to the C-suite: chief cultural officer. People in this new role are responsible for ensuring new employees clearly understand the organization's mission, strategy, and values, and equally important, how they work together to please their customers. A popular strategy is immersing new hires in comprehensive orientation programs.

> Look at a well-run company, and you will see the needs of its stockholders, its employees, and the community at large being served simultaneously.
>
> —ARNOLD HIATT, FORMER CEO, STRIDE RITE

Instead of doing any technical work during the first week on the job at MailChimp, new hires mostly experience the cultural aspects of the work environment. They are given company-logoed items and taken on tours to meet team members from different departments. Each department gives a high-level overview of how their part of the organization delivers on customer needs. Sometimes veteran employees cheer the new hires as they come through their work area. Before the end of the week, new hires use the same MailChimp app as customers. GlassDoor reports consistently show five-star ratings from MailChimp employees. Customers give good reviews of the company as well.

United Airlines created a commercial advertisement ahead of the Winter Olympic and Paralympic Games in Pyeongchang, South Korea, in part to help their employees understand why their work matters. The ad shows two types of superheroes: six US Olympic and Paralympic athletes sponsored by United (official airline of Team USA) and six United employees responsible for transporting competitors and their gear to the Games and back. Superhero nicknames are used to refer to Olympic events and United jobs. When a transportation problem occurs in the ad, an Olympian says, "*We* can't fly. But you know who can—the helpful crew at United, of course! They'll get our Olympic heroes to the games on time!" Mark Krolick, vice president of marketing at United says, "The tie between superheroes and Team USA athletes is clear. They are regular people who use their exceptional talents to accomplish the incredible."

> Keep the right goal in mind: Don't look for money, look for applause. If you create something of value, the sales will come.
>
> —ROBERT RONSTADT,
> CEO,
> LORD PUBLISHING

For years, Adobe focused on building a strong employee experience. After realizing that customers drive the business, the company changed the focus to "be as great to work with as it is to work for." They believe that both notions go hand in hand. Engaged workers strive to do their best, and customers feel more satisfied.

CASE STUDY: THE VALUE OF A CAUSE-DRIVEN MISSION

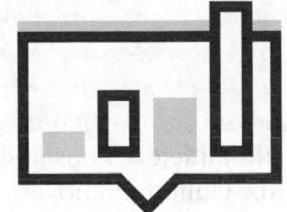

Says CEO Mark Luciano:

At NeuVanta, our work culture is embedded with the philosophy that we are part of this company to serve a higher cause. And that is to make a difference in the lives of people with Parkinson's, a debilitating neurological disorder. Everything that we do is to serve our target population and help "Create a Better You." Every employee understands that their work and effort is going to help people affected by this disease. Whether it is creating an e-learning course on older adult balance, to providing an Engineering PE Exam course for engineers to earn their professional license, we are helping people and servicing a great need.

Adds Ann Boland, executive for business development:

We focus employees on our logo statement, "Create a Better You." We actively evaluate any new product in terms of how it can be positioned within this statement. There isn't a long-winded mission statement, just four words on which to focus. We also surround ourselves with can-do people. Whether that is fellow employees, contractors, clients—attitude is everything. If a problem seems out of your control or insurmountable, have every involved employee respond to the question, "Well, what can we do?" As often as not, the problem will be solved or mitigated.

Mark continues:

Having a purpose to serve and make a difference has created loyalty and a can-do attitude, and most importantly, team collaboration on setting and meeting goals. Granted we are small with seven employees, but we have had zero turnover of employees since we started four years ago. The number-one reason employees cite for staying with the company was "serving a higher need." Our cause-driven company has also allowed us to attract top outside executives for our board of directors to help govern and provide guidance to the company.

Since we are cause driven, the engagement of employees comes from a "higher calling." But even with a strong sense of mission, it's still a business dealing with human beings and human nature, so the company has additional strategies to help keep people engaged. We find that it is a mixture of things that keep employees engaged. One style doesn't fit all.

We try to be flexible to meet the individual needs of the employee:

→ *Every employee is a stockholder in the company. This creates a sense of being part of something that may pay off good dividends in the future. It makes the employees think like an owner.*

→ *Our management style follows the Montessori method, that is, rules are set at a higher level and moderately controlled by management, but at the lower level, employees are free to roam within their space to solve customer problems as long as they stay within the high-level rules. They usually resolve problems before I knew that there was one.*

→ *We have 100 percent accessibility to management. We have an open-door policy. Any employee at any time can request a meeting with management to discuss concerns or just be updated on a current event.*

→ *As the CEO, I send employees an essay every year to start out the New Year. I try to get their thought processes going. For example, one year I wrote an essay entitled "Fate Favors the Fearless," which was actually taken from a fortune cookie I had. The next year it was "You Have a Right to Question Management on Anything and So Do They," with the point being that we are a transparent company. We have to be because everyone is a stockholder.*

→ We don't have a set policy for vacations days, sick days, or holidays. The rules are simple: thirty days off, ten company holidays with pay, twenty days to use however you want (vacation, sick, child sick, and so on).

→ We have flexible working hours, or as I call it, a free-to-roam policy. There are no eight-to-five jobs here. You can work from 6 A.M. to noon, and if you have everything under control and need the afternoon off to drive your daughter to a gymnastics meet one state over, that's okay with us. We do ask for permission in advance and that you are accessible by phone or email during normal business hours. If this person's unit is not performing, however, we may clamp down a bit and curtail this activity.

Adobe analyzed their work processes to better connect the employee and customer experience. According to Donna Morris, executive vice president of customer and employee experience, many organizations will find it is easier to align core mechanisms with their experience model. When both employees and customers use the same products, employees tend to become customers as well. As part of its strategy, Adobe encourages employees to advocate on the customers' behalf. For example, any employee can report a problem as soon as it arises, so it can be fixed well ahead of a customer who might experience and complain about it later.

To see where things are improving and where corrections may be needed, Adobe regularly surveys employees about their engagement levels with the company and with customers.

Premier Nutrition Corporation based in Emeryville, California, helps employees stay aware of its mission, strategy, and performance in a fun way. The nutrition company holds an all-hands meeting every Monday at 9 A.M. During the meeting, people and departments update each other while they sip and enjoy the Morning Protein Boost—the latest shake recipe. The staff reviews the past week's successes and challenges and what's coming next. They also highlight team members' professional and personal achievements. A state of the company meeting occurs quarterly where year-to-date revenues and earnings are reviewed. Then, the entire company engages in a fun activity such as a bike ride over the Golden Gate Bridge. Encouraging employees to recommend innovative ideas is another way they keep a focus on what is important. They've suggested and/or managed new projects from Doggy Day at work to starting philanthropies. "When you put all of these elements together, you get a community that challenges you professionally, yet supports you emotionally and even physically," says company president Darcy Horn Davenport. "PNC was recently certified as a Great Place to Work. We're extremely proud because it's based on feedback from current employees."

At Citigroup, the financial services firm headquartered in New York, more than 100,000 of the company's employees participate in a company-wide performance management system, with managers tracking goals—and tracking employee performance against the goals. Citigroup has developed a series of competencies and attributes linked to its core values, known as its shared responsibilities, which include such things as providing clients with superior products and services and always acting with the highest level of integrity. The company holds all managers accountable through the performance management system for delivering these attributes and competencies.

Allied Irish Bank closed seventy branches and laid off 13,000 people after the Great Recession. To drive commitment for a recovery, the bank ran a Gallup engagement survey, helped leaders understand their scores, and helped them learn skills to improve those scores. They also shared best practice stories, provided one-to-one coaching for  700 leaders to help engage their teams, and hosted an online "brand jam" to get employee input. These strategies helped drive ownership of the brand values. The bank also refreshed the tone of voice of its internal communications, going from extremely formal legalese to more positive, future focused, simple, and human. Overall engagement changed from 81 percent to 86 percent, the greatest increase in Europe that the Gallup organization has ever seen. Absenteeism also dropped, saving €1.2 million.

The point is that you always have to maintain credibility. That requires a sixth sense, one that tells you when your credibility is in question. You know it. You can hear it out on the shop floor. You can feel it. To be a good manager, you have to have that sixth sense.

—JACK STACK, CEO, SRC

Accellent, a leading medical device supplier and maker of small parts for heart transplant catheters and surgical instruments, with fourteen manufacturing facilities in twelve American states as well as operations in Germany, Ireland, Mexico, the United Kingdom, and  South Korea struggled with employees understanding all the good things the company was doing. To address this need, Accellent interviewed patients who had used some of their products, created posters that featured the patients' faces and personal stories, and put them up in all of their offices. The effect has been amazing. Overall engagement has continued to increase year after year, due in part to the fact that people truly understand the good their work is doing. Says Tricia McCall, senior vice president of human resources:

It started a conversation. People understood that they were making a difference. Quality and performance improved. We asked, "How do you get folks to never take a shortcut, to always do their best work?" You help them think about what they're making and how important it is.

Do all workers understand the mission of the company, the philosophy of senior management? To really feel included in the corporate culture, workers should know why the company exists, its basic values, and the ways in which it cares for its customers.

—RICHARD ROSS,
PRESIDENT,
TRI COMPANIES

CASE STUDY:
CREATING A NOBLE CAUSE CAN
DRIVE ENGAGEMENT

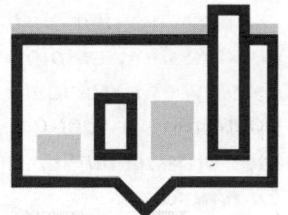

William B. Luciano, executive vice president of NeuKinetics Wellness (a division of NeuVanta) offers his thoughts on employee engagement:

The cornerstone to engaging employees is to find a way for your company to exist for a cause higher than just profits. I call it a noble cause. This noble cause drives great workforce job satisfaction, which creates overall happiness within its coworkers, which in turn circles back to strong workforce engagement. There is no better example than our company, NeuVanta, which is dedicated to helping those with Parkinson's, a devastating neurological disease that makes everyday activities like walking extremely difficult.

There's a remarkable sense of accomplishment in being a part of a company and program that can alter the progression of Parkinson's for the millions of people with the disease. But not many companies can have such an altruistic mission. Or can they?

For many, working for a company that offers high salaries and generous benefits would be an easy decision. After all, big salaries should create workforce happiness, which should create job satisfaction and engagement within the company—right? Wrong. Without a noble cause as part of an organization's mission, the motivational effects of money on employees quickly wear off. They want more money, and when that isn't forthcoming, they become disengaged. We need money to live, and certainly there is a threshold of monetary reward the company must meet for its employees, and sharing in the overall success of the company is equally important. However, money alone will never create an engaged workforce, but having a noble cause will.

So how could a company continue to create a feeling of engagement among its employees? Here is what we do:

First, we demonstrate how pleased customers are with our product. We show employees letters of appreciation from customers. Our employees participate in customer and supplier focus groups to help shape the services we provide, and we show them how the products they produce are creating a better world. This can be very rewarding for employees.

Second, we have a workforce that is incredibly connected with our product line on a personal, one-to-one level. This is powerful because every employee is touched personally by the market we serve. Everyone knows a family member, friend, or neighbor that is affected by Parkinson's or older adult balance issues. There are 1.5 million people with Parkinson's disease, and another 17 million who experience balance problems that result in falls over the age of sixty-five. The more employees are personally engaged, the more they begin to care about the job they do and better serve external and internal clients. And in some small way, they begin to reflect on what this company means to all their coworker friends, and how their own job contribution truly matters.

Third, we have a company culture that truly cares about the people it serves. The company and its employees need to give of themselves—their time and toil—by volunteering. And it all starts at the top. Management in our company voluntarily serve on local Parkinson's boards. For lower-income areas, we often donate our program to a local Parkinson's group to use for exercise programs. By giving more of our time, caring more about the market we serve, there truly is no better feeling in the world than to be part of a company that rallies around a personal cause for a person or group of people in need.

Research has demonstrated that human interaction creates the most happiness, whether it's close family bonds, best friends, or strong workforce ties. I've been in sales all my life. I know, when I walk into a client's office, I'm representing everyone

> Whatever your culture, values, and guiding principles, you have to take steps to inculcate them in the organization early in its life to guide every decision, every hire, every strategic objective.
>
> —HOWARD SCHULTZ, CEO, STARBUCKS

in the company. It's a powerful incentive to do my best because I know they depend on me, as well as their families! Every individual within the company has that same level of job responsibility to each other and should feel the same. And leadership conveys this message. As leaders, we must make sure they understand that each person in the organization is truly responsible in some way for everyone else in the company. The personal ties really drive home this point, make it believable, and make the company's work meaningful—

> A business has to be involving, it has to be fun, and it has to exercise your creative instincts.
>
> —SIR RICHARD BRANSON, FOUNDER, THE VIRGIN GROUP

and that is what engages employees. So as a leader, make it a point to have your employees really get to know each other. The culture of leadership maintaining an arms-length relationship with their employees is dead. When employees truly care about each other, they will naturally become engaged in the common bond of their company— for the betterment of their coworkers, themselves, and ultimately, the business.

Gracious Space: Spirit, Setting, Inviting the "Stranger," and Learning in Public

At Hearthstone, a retirement living facility located in Seattle, Washington, they have a yearly theme to help drive the focus of all members of the organization. The theme for the previous year was "Be kinder than necessary." The current year's theme is "Show your gratitude." John Paulson, the organization's chief human resource officer, says the themes help to engage employees to "bring their best self" to work every day. "I found the Center for Ethical Leadership's concept of gracious space to be an excellent training tool to elevate our 'serve' philosophy and allow all of us an opportunity to truly reach our potential." Here is a brief synopsis:

Spirit:
Intentionally Create a Supportive Environment

Gracious space calls forth attributes such as compassion, curiosity, and humor that we each embody. When we bring these attributes with us into relationships, we are "being" gracious space. The spirit of gracious space includes the *spirit you bring,* the *spirit of the group,* and *tapping into a greater spirit* of the work. The spirit of gracious space helps us to be the change we want to see in the world.

Setting:
Pay Attention to the Physical Environment

Gracious space has a physical dimension that can support or impede our ability to work with others. By paying attention to simple hospitality, comfort, and the diversity or history of a place, you can create a thoughtful setting of gracious space. Setting includes ensuring the *approach complements your goal* and being intentional about *adding items that can enhance* gracious space.

Invite the "Stranger":
Intentionally Seek the Other

This is the willingness and ability to welcome the other and seek out people, ideas, and perspectives—even if these are different, inconvenient, or uncomfortable. Inviting the stranger asks us to determine *who we need in the room, who or what is the stranger or strange idea,* and what we can *learn from the stranger.* We need the stranger when considering complex and new ideas, lest we take narrow-minded or short-term actions. It's helpful to remember we are each the stranger to someone else.

Learn in Public:
Let Go and Open Up to Possibility

In gracious space, people listen more and judge less. Learning in public asks us to *suspend judgment, take risks,* and *pay attention to our learning.* It asks us to see difference as an opportunity to learn something new. In this space, we can work better across boundaries, share diverse perspectives, work through conflict, discover transformative solutions, and carry out innovations for change.

To Create Gracious Space

- → Bring your spirit.

- → Attend to the physical setting.

- → Invite the "stranger."

- → Learn together.

5

JOB CONTENT

Managers often overlook elements of the work itself
that can be highly motivating to employees: autonomy,
flexibility, and challenge to name but a few such elements.

Employees need to know what is expected of them and to be
given the opportunity to do what they do best every day at
work. All performance thus starts with clear goals and expectations. How you set goals for your employees is important, not just
for clarity as to what needs to be done, but also for the motivational
value it can add for the employee if you do it right. The best goal-setting
has three common elements:

1. **The best goals are few in number, specific in purpose.** Even with all the talk about multitasking, ultimately a person can focus on only one thing at a time. So the greater the number of goals you have, the less likely any of those goals will get worked on, let alone finished.

2. **The best goals are not too easy and not too hard.** If a goal is too easy, we tend to not even try to do it. If it's too difficult and we don't think we can achieve it, this also inhibits our efforts to attempt the task. The best goals are somewhere in between these two extremes, some say ideally having a 70 percent chance of completion.

3. **The best goals are collaborative in nature.** The days of telling employees what to do are over. You need to discuss goals with employees and get their input to get their buy in to make them *their* goals. Otherwise, you're less likely to get their best effort. If you can link the goal to something you know is of interest to the employee, all the better.

As management theorist Frederick Herzberg put it, "If you want someone to do a good job, give them a good job to do." Find out what tasks your employees most enjoy and excel at, and use that information to link them to relevant needs of the organization.

By allowing your employees flexibility in setting their own priorities, in the specifics of how they handle their work, or even in their choice of working hours you can establish a relationship of trust and respect instead of "my way or the highway." To the extent that managers of the organization are able to provide those motivators for employees, their employees' level of engagement will be greatly impacted, and they'll be better able to do the best work possible.

> If it makes sense, we should probably allow it.
>
> —JEFF WEINER, CEO, LINKEDIN

In my research into what most motivates employees at work, "flexibility of working hours" was one of the top motivators for today's employees. Many managers and companies have found that giving employees the options of a flexible schedule or telecommuting has increased employee engagement. For some, the attraction is less time spent commuting each week and saving money on gas or mileage. Others may find it beneficial to limit childcare expenses or simply to have the opportunity to spend more time with their families. Whatever the motivation, employees appreciate the option of being able to have some control over their own work and, as a result, feel as though the company has their best interests in mind. Other options for increasing flexibility include:

→ Alternate hours (arriving early and leaving early or vice versa).

→ Four-day work weeks, in which longer hours are worked on fewer days.

→ Telecommuting.

→ Job sharing.

→ Allowing an employee to leave work early when necessary or take time off to compensate for extra hours worked.

Following are other examples of how the job itself can serve to better engage employees.

> People want to learn new things, to feel they've made a contribution—that they are doing worthwhile work. Few people are motivated only by money. People want to feel that what they do makes a difference in the world.
>
> —FRANCES HESSELBEIN,
> PRESIDENT, LEADER TO LEADER

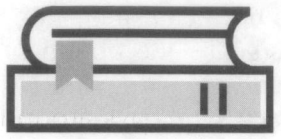 Entertainment agency ZinePak empowers its employees to manage their own time, including working remotely. Cofounder Kim Kaupe says employees are more invested in getting the work done as efficiently as possible, something they were not achieving by making sure they were in their chairs by 9 A.M.

At Johnson County Government, seated in Olathe, Kansas, departments are empowered to operate in ways that work for them. An "Employee Engagement Best Practices Playbook" helps guide each individual and each department with their planning.

Gaming software company Valve asks employees to help make a "crazy" handbook for new hires. Employees contribute funny drawings and phrases.

Marco Bizzari, CEO of Gucci, says, "The person making decisions should be the one with the most knowledge, not the most senior person, and that could be a twenty-five-year-old kid." To get a different and fresh perspective, Bizzari regularly confers with two committees, Comex and Shadow Comex, whose members are under the age of thirty.

Richard Knowles, a former plant manager for chemical manufacturer E.I. du Pont de Nemours in Belle, West Virginia, found that when he set goals for his employees, he often set them too low. He therefore stopped doing so, instead relying on them to donate their discretionary energy when they found meaning in their work.

By way of its results-only work environment (ROWE), consumer electronics retailer Best Buy of Richfield, Minnesota, allows employees to decide for themselves where, when, and how they work as long as they get results. Employees start and end their workdays around a core set of hours and are given complete freedom to determine their own schedules. According to the company, productivity has increased 35 percent for employees working in the ROWE program—which will save the company approximately $13 million per year when all 4,000 employees are brought into the system.

At online music powerhouse Pandora Media, founder and chief strategy officer Tim Westergren pushed decision-making authority down to Pandora's workforce. The result is a strong culture of employee involvement and engagement where coworkers develop deep and long-lasting bonds with their coworkers. When new employees arrive for their first day of work, they are taken through an orientation process that introduces Pandora's culture to them—including making decisions with the smallest number of people possible. According to Westergren, the results of Pandora's approach has been quite positive for the company: "You become much more nimble. So you are able to make decisions quickly. It saves people time and makes them more efficient, which makes them happier. It also gives people a real sense of ownership."

Involving individuals in the business is the most effective way to produce an organization in which people know more, care more, and do the right things.

—EDWARD LAWLER III,
PROFESSOR,
UNIVERSITY OF
SOUTHERN CALIFORNIA

Jorge Perez—founder, chairman, and CEO of The Related Group, a construction firm located in Miami, Florida—feels that creating a culture where he can entrust his employees with making even the most important decisions for the company is essential for its long-term growth. According to Perez, there are a few things organizations can do to ensure they have the right people with the right decision-making skills on board:

> → **Hire tough.** Perez's philosophy is that if you hire tough, then you manage easy. You have to take the time required to find and hire stars.

> → **Create a personal road map.** Establish each employee's goals and parameters, then provide praise and corrections along the way.

> → **Dole out more risk.** Give employees progressively more authority—and risk—the longer they are with the company and the more they show they are able to handle it. As Perez says, "Give them the keys to the scooter before the keys to the Harley."

Employees at Park Ridge Hospital in Hendersonville, North Carolina, are given the authority to issue patients apologies and small-denomination gift cards when there are glitches in service delivery, such as having to wait several hours for tests when the required equipment breaks.

At Internet services company Google, engineers are given permission to devote up to 20 percent of their time to doing projects of their own choosing. Products resulting from this policy include Gmail, Google News, Orkut, Google Sky, and Google Grants.

Online retailer Zappos empowers call-center service agents to use their judgment to do whatever it takes to delight the company's customers without the prewritten scripts and time limits typical for most call centers. The company's annual revenues are fast approaching $2 billion.

Outdoor clothing manufacturer Patagonia of Ventura, California, allows employees to make personalized work schedules that enable them to pursue their interests during the course of a typical workday, which might include surfing in the morning or taking a hike in the afternoon. Not only are employees more engaged with their employer, but they are more connected to the products the company sells.

> We have challenges—but they always make us better and stronger.
>
> —MARK PARKER, CEO, NIKE

Employees at incentive company Achievers in Toronto, Ontario, get to lead the vision committee of their choice. Members of committees devote about one day a week to work on committee goals, which can range from revising the company dress code to creating new marketing campaigns. When the company moved into a new space three times larger than the one they were leaving behind, members of its Culture Up the Office group were tasked with conceptualizing the employee break area, including updates on company and work-unit goals.

Auto parts manufacturer Dana Corporation of Toledo, Ohio, requires each of its employees to make at least two suggestions for improvement each month. If the changes proposed would cost the company less than $500, then the employees do not need permission from the plant manager to put them into effect themselves. The program, known as Bright Ideas, has saved Dana millions of dollars.

> I think our story proves there's absolutely no limit to what plain, ordinary, working people can accomplish if they're given the opportunity and encouragement to do their best.
>
> —SAM WALTON,
> FOUNDER, WALMART

Individual stores within the Flight Centre UK travel agency, headquartered in the United Kingdom, are encouraged to consider themselves semiautonomous businesses within the larger organization. Each of the store's six or seven employees takes on different roles, such as marketing, finance, and customer service. Managing director Chris Galanty reports that employees feel like they are managing their own business, while developing new skills along the way. "This is a customer-facing company, and better-engaged staff give better service and make more money."

Everyone is encouraged to "work like they own the company" at Hilcorp Energy, and "decision-making is pushed to the front lines." Cash buy-in plans allow workers to own a piece of the company's projects and eventual profits, which staffers say rewards hard work. As a result, employees receive annual bonuses that average about 36 percent of their salary, but 60 percent is not unusual.

To consistently review online customer feedback, New York jewelry company BaubleBar created a dedicated team called SWAT (service with accessorizing talent). Company cofounder Daniella Yacobovsky says, "Once a customer was upset because earrings she needed to wear as a bridesmaid had sold out. A SWAT stylist tracked down a sample pair and rushed the package to her."

According to Ilir Sela, founder and CEO of Slice, the company is in the business of ordering pizza. Sela says, "Early on, if a customer complained about food, we'd direct them to the restaurant—we thought we only had to own the ordering component. But we have to own the full experience." The company now solves customer issues with both the computer and the restaurants. Slice employees leave online complaints as they are reported and respond directly to them online. Anyone can see how problems are resolved.

Companies like Genentech, Georgetown University Hospitals, and Hermann Miller have employees shaping their work by allocating chunks of discretionary time to pursue projects of their own choosing. Holly Butler, senior staffing manager for Genentech's research group, says, "Discretionary time is a huge piece of why they want to work at Genentech. It is Disneyland for scientists."

To encourage more innovation and enjoyment at work, Scott Farquhar and Mike Cannon-Brookes, founders of Australian software firm Atlassian, asked employees to devote one workday toward solving any problem, as long as it was not connected to their official role. As a result, Atlassian developed new products and was able to resolve issues with existing ones. The program is now a fundamental part of the Atlassian work environment.

> The need to pay more attention to quality and productivity is another reason for frontline workers' increased involvement in production decisions. Flexible, highly skilled employees can provide better service than do workers who can offer only narrow specialized service.
>
> —RAY MARSHALL, FORMER US SECRETARY OF LABOR

Because of unhappy employees and an annual turnover rate of 35 percent at St. Lucie Medical Center in Florida, executive leadership analyzed the capabilities and responsibilities of its workforce. They completed talent inventories and developed ideas to better build and align teams. The result: Overall attrition rates dropped significantly after two years. It dropped almost 50 percent for nursing roles. Physician satisfaction scores also improved, going up by 72 percent. Patient satisfaction increased 160 percent compared to similar hospitals.

Toyota's North American Parts Center inadvertently shifted into a traditional Western supervisor-employee culture within a year and a half of starting operations in California. To change this cultural orientation, the company sent all managers to a four-day workshop to become aware of each person's talent assets and to plan ways to better apply their talents to individual and team situations. In addition, warehouse employees participated in Learn at Lunch meetings to develop plans to use their talents more effectively. The overall result for the entire employee population of 400 workers on fifty-four teams: Productivity increased 6 percent after the first year. Productivity went up 9 percent for workshop participants.

....

There are no managers or hierarchy at video-game developer Valve. Employees work directly with one another. New hires are selected by committees, and anyone can work on any project in the company. There are peer reviews for bonuses and disciplinary actions. The result: The company is now worth $4.1 billion.

....

You get a sense that you own the business. That means you're going to spend a lot less time worrying about whose toes you're going to tread on and much more time worrying about how you're going to move that business forward.

—JAMES A. MEEHAN,
MANAGER,
GENERAL ELECTRIC

At each Costco store, the big-box giant based in Issaquah, Washington, employees are given great autonomy. Warehouse managers have authority to recruit and manage their staffs with little oversight from corporate headquarters. There are written management guidelines. Every three years, employees give feedback on the guidelines, which often results in improvements.

....

Gensler, the architectural firm based in San Francisco, provides employees with greater control over their physical workspace. Employee surveys resulted in more innovation, greater job satisfaction and performance, and improved focus for people working in open-space areas.

To help design new company uniforms, Alaska Airlines surveyed thousands of employees to get their preferences, needs, and suggestions. Many focus groups were also held. More than anything, employees asked for more pockets and timeless silhouettes that flattered a variety of body types. To accommodate the ever-changing climates the airline crews travel to, the new uniforms are designed to be layered.

> My goal is to give them the tools to succeed. But I hold them accountable to execute our business plans.
>
> —STEPHEN HOLMES, CHAIRMAN AND CEO, WYNDHAM WORLDWIDE

At Xerox, one customer service center turned decisions about work schedules over to the employees. With employee work teams in charge of the scheduling, the company reported higher morale, better customer service, and a 30 percent reduction in absenteeism.

Reference International Software in San Francisco allows one day a week for customer service reps to work on any project they choose. Some results have included better systems and new, salable products, in addition to greatly enhanced employee morale.

The president of Pizza Hut asked employees how to eliminate needless paperwork and tasks and improve their working conditions. The result was a company with fewer layers of management, less corporate paperwork, and a 40 percent growth in sales.

At Nucor, executives say almost all of the best new ideas come from the factory floor, and new hires often come up with them. Because of this, the newest workers are sent to existing plants to hunt for improvement opportunities and, longer-term workers are sent to newly acquired plants to see what they can learn from them. To minimize layers of management, Nucor has pushed work that used to be done by supervisors, such as ordering parts, down to line workers and pushed the duties of plant managers down to supervisors. CEO DiMicco says his executive vice presidents are like "mini CEOs, and he is their board."

Charlene Pedrolie, manufacturing chief at Virginia's Rowe Furniture Company, believed that the people doing the work should design how the work is done. They moved from an environment in which each person handled part of a process to fully cross-trained manufacturing cells producing a whole product.

At Ohio's Monarch Marking Systems, managers instituted a "small set of simple rules" to change the mindset of employees. They required people to participate on teams formed specifically to improve a particular performance metric. Teams were allowed no more than thirty days to form the team, study a problem, and implement a solution. More than 100 teams have met with success and improved the organization's engagement scores.

Edward Jones, the fourth-largest financial advisory firm in the United States, was facing a cost-cutting dilemma: Cut jobs or find other ways to save $100 million to offset lost revenue. The company turned to its associates to come up with cost-saving ideas. Management picked the best ideas. When the results were tallied, the company saved $120 million—and gained the commitment of its people.

Case Study:
Making Unglamorous
Work Engaging

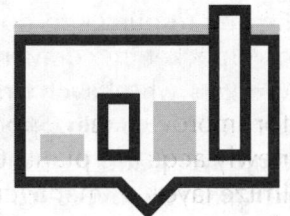

Often, a manager thinks, "But the work we need to have done is *boring* and unexciting. How can that work be made to *engage* employees?" The first step is to at least try. Kevin Sheridan, a leading employee engagement expert, shares the example of just such work in his book *Building a Magnetic Culture*.

Susan Young, director of Minneapolis Solid Waste and Recycling, has worked for the City of Minneapolis, Minnesota, for over twenty years. She is quick to boast that her city has been ranked the fifth cleanest city in the world. Young oversees 158 direct employees as well as a very large base of contract workers. She says her employees are engaged for a myriad of reasons, including that "expectations are very clear here. A clean city is a job well done."

Young's staff members enjoy the stability of an industry that will always be needed. However, Young says they earn their jobs every day, since they are one of the only cities in Minnesota that does not outsource waste management services. If they continue to be successful in providing cost-effective service for their city, their jobs will not be lost to an outside company. Job security is a major retention factor for employees, and they work hard because they feel their fate is in their own hands.

Many of Young's employees are independent workers who enjoy being in a field where "someone isn't looking over their shoulder all the time." Staff members have the autonomy to go out and do what needs to be done, and go home when they are finished. This freedom motivates employees to work hard so they can end their shifts early and have a more positive work-life balance.

Employees are motivated by their role in making Minneapolis a great place to live. They can actively see the difference their jobs make, and that evokes a sense of pride in their work. Young also wants to motivate her staff through monetary rewards but has limited resources to do so. She gives a small cash award out of her own pocket in a drawing once a year at the annual employee event. Workers who haven't missed more than a couple of shifts that year are eligible to win. She finds this to be a great way to reward her top employees and to show them she personally cares about them as people. Employees truly value working for the City of Minneapolis, and some have been on board for thirty years.

6

SENIOR MANAGEMENT'S RELATIONSHIP WITH EMPLOYEES

More executives can talk the talk—but walking the walk matters most to employees.

It's no secret that the effectiveness of most organizations emulates from the quality and focus of its senior leaders, starting with the organization's CEO. As such, it is critical for senior leadership of an organization to be visible and openly "walk the talk" as to what's most important for everyone to focus on and why. This requires an active, visible role among the employee population. In fact, "upper management visibility" and "concern for employees" have a near perfect correlation in research on employee engagement.

The relationship between upper management and employees is also critical to drive the mission and strategies of the organization. I once heard Jeff Immelt make a public presentation when he was

CEO of General Electric. Someone asked him, "In your position as the CEO of a major corporation, how do you get everyone moving in the same direction?" Mr. Immelt responded, "Well, I'll tell you how to NOT do it. You can't announce the company is going to be an ISO9000-certified supplier and then go into your office for six months to then emerge and ask 'How's that ISO9000 certification coming?' because it won't be happening. For those things that are most important for the business, you have to get on the horse and ride it."

This chapter will show examples of what active senior management and visibility look like in organizations today.

When he was CEO of Ford Motor Company, Alan Mulally had all members of his executive team each invite two employees to their executive meetings. This both encouraged transparency and helped everyone to be on their best behavior as well.

> You have to be good with people. Get the best people, make sure they are properly motivated, and give them a lot of freedom to make good things and make mistakes.
>
> —SIR RICHARD BRANSON,
> FOUNDER AND CHAIRMAN,
> THE VIRGIN GROUP

On most Friday afternoons at Coinbase in San Francisco, California, CEO Brian Armstrong convenes an informal meeting in the company cafeteria. He encourages employees to drop by to raise an issue or ask a question about any part of the business.

Elon Musk, founder and CEO of SpaceX, regularly sends encouraging emails and gives inspiring speeches to his employees. He has also invited famous people such as George Takei and Jeremy Edberg to address his workforce.

Whenever possible, Doug Herbert, president of Herbert Construction Company in Metro Atlanta stops into the new employee orientation to briefly talk with new employees, thanks them for joining the company, and shares the three main behaviors they can do to be successful at our company:

1. **Be productive**. If they are asked to get lumber from the truck, bring back five pieces in one trip instead of making five trips.

2. **Keep learning**. Primarily unskilled and inexperienced, they need to learn what we do and why. Then they can take on more responsibility, become more valuable, and make more money.

3. **Be safe**. Ask for help when they need it (such as when lifting heavy items). Watch out for the safety of coworkers.

If employees have questions, issues, or suggestions, Herbert encourages them to come talk with him. "When they see the president of the company thanks them for joining the company, and makes himself available to them," says Herbert, "I think they feel more connected to their new company."

Michael Tatelbame, vice president of human resources for Villa Healthcare in Skokie, Illinois, reports:

As part of my servant leadership work, I've been very focused on Stephen Covey's speed of trust concept: connect-trust-act. Dr. Covey talks about the importance of taking time to connect with others, to build trust, and then move to action. Leaders (and others) tend to move right to action. At Villa, I've implemented Coffee Talks, a chance for me to explain the concept and live it by connecting with our corporate staff. These Coffee Talks are limited to six corporate staff at a time. Offered monthly, staff voluntarily sign up, but there's a buzz in the office and staff wait and watch for the sign-up sheet each month.

We all take time to share at the level each person is most comfortable. I talk about the power of vulnerability, that everyone has a story. As a result, the group realizes how we are more similar than different. Right now, only I am doing these, but soon we will expect our facility leaders to do Coffee Talks with their staff. It's extremely powerful in so many ways.

When Heather Machado was chair of the nursing recruitment and retention team at Hartford Hospital in Connecticut, they developed an initiative called the Sixty-Day Hire to ensure new nurse hires had a voice with senior leadership early on in their career. An onboarding survey was sent at the sixty-day mark to understand the experiences of new nurses. At the ninety-day mark, the new nurse hires were invited to a breakfast or luncheon in their honor to explore and gather feedback regarding their onboarding experience. "Nursing senior leadership attended to hear feedback, and I served as the facilitator," says Machado.

We used classical music, a "Welcome" place mat, candles, and balloons to set the tone. Using our ten leadership behaviors and core values, we were able to save twenty-five new nurses within the first *year just by listening, acknowledging, and taking action. The result was a 95 percent retention rate the first year for those who attended, and a $1.6 million dollar savings in turnover.*

A new graduate nurse program was adopted later. The initiative protocol and results were presented at the state and national level. Our major finding was—relationships matter:

→ *The relationship with the direct nurse manager matters.*

→ *The relationship with the health-care team matters and is important when assimilating into a new environment.*

→ *Nurses need the resources and tools to do their job.*

→ *A streamlined orientation specific to their work environment is critical.*

→ *Improvements were made based on their feedback.*

The Granite Group, based in Concord, New Hampshire, has thirty-four locations and nearly 500 employees in six states. "Our competitive advantage is our people and we pride ourselves on having a well-trained and very knowledgeable team," says Tracie Sponenberg, senior vice president of human resources. "Our business and our culture is relationship driven, and the members of our senior leadership team help foster that relationship-driven culture."

As part of their normal job responsibilities, senior members are required to regularly visit each branch. This promotes a connection to geographically separated branches and people, and also aids in the trust the team has in senior management—something many organizations struggle with. "In particular, our CEO Bill Condron spends a significant time in the branches," adds Sponenberg. "He can walk into any of our locations at any time, without flustering any of the team members, and he knows each employees' name, which means a lot to them!"

Matt Dwyer, president of Dwyer Engineering in Leesburg, Virginia, writes:

I had been trying to get an organized activity started in my company for team building, but I couldn't get it off top dead center. I thought I had good ideas (baseball games, sailing), but they did not seem popular with the staff. They all involved weekends, which is when I had free time, and they all involved activities I like. I could tell that enthusiasm was muted to say the least, and I didn't want to spend $100 to $150 per person (I include families or significant others in company events we do) for something that was perceived as a duty. Another senior staff member took a stab at it, and again, it pretty much went nowhere.

I learned I was guilty of having the best intentions, poorly executed. Like many companies, we planned team-building reward activities that center around the boss's favorite activities (e.g., golf), then scheduled those on a day that is good for the boss but very inconvenient for a number of employees. This becomes an unappreciated burden, even if the boss pays for everything.

We changed course and turned it over to a young employee who was excited about taking charge. By letting the enthusiastic "kids" in the office plan the event, it completely changed everything. We just gave them a budget, included families as an option, asked them to get buy-in from a majority, and retained veto rights (naked mud wrestling is probably not happening). That person met with other employees his age and came up with a list of their own ideas. I nixed one of those ideas, and they surveyed everyone to get a sense of what was the most popular and most inclusive (not always the same thing) using SurveyMonkey. They then used Doodle to find a good date for everyone. They put it all together, and we wound up doing a medieval dinner and joust night on a Friday evening for a few hours. Some staff with small children brought them, and they sat us all together. The staff made a big deal about us. The whole process galvanized the younger staff put in charge of it and we have repeated the process with success multiple times. The last event was at Top Golf, a local semi-indoor golf game that includes dinner and drinks.

It is always ironic when senior staff do something out of a sense of duty and then get annoyed at lack of appreciation. The younger staff, on the other hand, saw it as an opportunity to shine and have fun as well, and we were happy to have them organize it for us; it just took us a while to realize that. They ended up doing things senior management never even considered but turned out to be lots of fun!

> Our business is utterly dependent upon getting our 180,000 people aligned and moving forward.
>
> —Brian Dunn, CEO, Best Buy

When Michele Moore, founder and CEO of Southwest Human Capital based in Albuquerque, New Mexico, worked at the CIA, her group chief would regularly invite line-level employees to the C-suite for breakfast. This worked very well because line-level employees were able to get the full focus of the leader before the work day began.

I've also seen this done where just one employee at a time is allowed this visit, and I think that is even better, simply because it allows for more direct dialogue. My favorite thing about this kind of program is that the leaders typically start by feeling as if they are sacrificing to do employees a "favor" and end up prioritizing this time because they learn so much from employees about what is going on within the company. It really maintains those open lines of communication that are so important for strategic alignment and morale.

At Northeast Alabama Regional Medical Center (RMC), based in Anniston, Alabama, with three hospitals in Anniston and Jacksonville, Alabama, senior management is doing several good things to better engage employees, reports Don Stuckey, a consultant working for the company.

Louis Bass, CEO of RMC, has a meeting once a month with all middle managers. At each meeting he invites one or a group of staff employees to the meeting to recognize for outstanding performance.

 How does he know whom to recognize? He gets input from "Dear CEO" boxes throughout the hospital, and he also makes rounds regularly and listens and observes. When he recognizes staff in front of middle management, he brings them to the front of the room, tells their story, and hands them an envelope with a gift card in it. Once a quarter, the executive team has multiple town hall–style meetings where each employee is invited and is informed on what is going on and how the company is doing.

Strategy and mission are very important at RMC, and there are several ways that employees learn about these. The executive team covers it in an orientation of all new employees. Signs are located in multiple places in the hospital. All employees are rated in their performance review regarding how they have contributed to the goals and live the vision: "To provide state-of-the-art health care with integrity to the people we serve."

Stuckey created a corporate university—RMC Academy—where midlevel managers are trained on about twenty different topics including engagement, recognition, selection, setting expectations, and so on.

Dale Dauten, author of many great leadership books including *The Gifted Boss* and *The Max Strategy*, shares a story about Charlie Hughes, who started the American division of Land Rover.

Hughes hosted a retreat for all employees to discuss the company's mission, strategy, and vision. Instead of the usual PowerPoint test of mental endurance, he decided to hold a Love the Product Day. He wanted to share with everyone the excitement of off-roading in a Range Rover, so he got his engineers to rent a backhoe and turn an empty field into an off-road test track. That driving experience was so powerful, it lead to the company creating test tracks at dealerships. After all, you want potential customers to have their own falling-in-love experience. Imagine if your company's mission was "To make products so good our customers love them and do the selling for us."

You might be thinking, "Well, sure, you can have a Love the Product event if you have a consumer product like a Range Rover." Think again. John Winzeler, CEO of Winzeler Gear, a thriving Chicago-based company that makes plastic parts, mostly for the auto industry, turned gears into something loveable:

➔ *He commissions gear art.*

➔ *He had a fashion designer create dresses made of gears.*

➔ *He has an art gallery in a gear factory.*

➔ *He's turned gears into key rings and earrings.*

That's loving the product, even when it seems unlovable. Whatever it is you sell, you have no excuse. If you can't love the product or the service you have to offer, either make it lovable or find a new place to work.

CASE STUDY: CULTURE BUILDING

CEO Munjal Shah of Health IQ, a life insurance startup based in Mountain View, California, maintains a personal commitment to three strategies to scale the work culture as his company grows.

1. **Interview job candidates.** "The faster a company is scaling, the more the CEO should be involved in hiring to ensure the quality of decisions is not only being maintained but elevated," says Shah. He interviews 90 percent of the job applicants.

2. **Democratize mentoring with open office hours.** "To scale quickly, help people grow professionally," says Shah, who holds weekly office hours. Anyone in the company can go see him.

3. **Recognize employees daily.** Shah notes, "The more recognition you give, the more positive your culture is. Appreciation never depreciates." Every afternoon the entire Health IQ team—many remotely connected via Skype—has a one-hour meeting to praise people for their accomplishments.

Leadership is all about convincing and motivating a group of people to do things they would not normally do in order to win.

—JOHN BROCK,
CHAIRMAN AND CEO, COCA-COLA

At Hireology, a hiring and talent management platform based in Chicago, Illinois, cofounder and CEO Adam Robinson and vice president of business development Kevin Baumgart know that saying things the right way can have big impact on employee development. In Corey Fein's initial position with the company, she had difficulty seeing meaningful results. The company had many metrics associated with her job. When it came to hard metrics like actual sales, the numbers didn't necessarily match her work efforts. After making over 900 calls during the first three weeks on the job, she did not see good results. That's when Adam and Kevin approached her. Fein says, "Instead of blaming me, they said, 'We're so proud of you for the effort you're putting in every day. We just know that the rest is going to fall into place.'" Their encouragement resulted in her wanting to perform better. She started to see great results within a few weeks after their conversation. Fein has since been promoted six times over a four-year period.

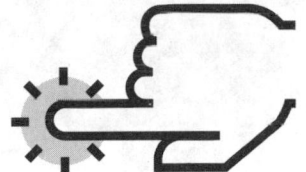

Treating his employees like family has helped Jeff Anon—founder, president, and CEO of Berryhill Baja Grill, a Mexican restaurant chain based in Houston, Texas—build an energized and productive workforce of more than 250 employees and annual sales of more than $22 million. Says Anon, "We get involved with their families. We support their Little League teams. We go to their weddings. It's a big, extended family that we have."

At SK Group, a conglomerate of energy, chemical, telecommunications, and trading companies in Seoul, Korea, executives regularly conduct forums with employees to keep them apprised about the company's ongoing successes and challenges, including SK's sales performance and growth.

Jeremiah Simmons, a McDonald's fast-food restaurant franchisee in the borough of Queens in New York City, understands the power of storytelling in inspiring his employees to the highest levels of performance. Says Simmons, "I tell all my crew when they come in that I started the way they started. They know my story. I was the hamburger flipper, the cashier, the guy with the mop." Simmons started out with McDonald's at age eighteen, doing all the things that entry-lev-

el employees do. Less than three years later, he had been promoted to store manager and increased the store's annual sales 44 percent to $3.9 million. Today, Simmons owns two McDonald's restaurants—and he has inspired many employees to follow his own example of dedication and enthusiasm.

Every Monday, Michael Yormark, president and COO of the Florida Panthers professional football team in Sunrise, Florida, holds a rally for the Panthers staff, and every morning he sends out a good-morning email message welcoming employees to work. Says Yormark, "I remind our staff that I have an open-door policy. And, from an employee's perspective, whether you're an entry-level employee or an employee that's been here for multiple years, you want to be able to feel that you can effect change in a company."

Chairman and CEO of First Chester County Corporation and First National Bank of Chester County in West Chester, Pennsylvania, John Featherman believes that making his company a fun place to work is a good way to engage his employees. Among other things, Featherman has been known to ride aboard First National's float in the local Christmas parade—wearing an Elvis jumpsuit. Says Featherman, "I try to be as visible as possible. For example, we hold our executive meetings once a week, and we move them around to different areas of the bank. I'll arrive early and talk with whoever's coming in to get coffee."

John Tisch, chairman and CEO of Loews Hotels in New York City agreed to appear on the popular TLC cable network television show *Now Who's Boss?* During the course of four days, he took on a variety of different frontline jobs in the Loews Miami Beach Hotel, including scrubbing bathrooms, cooking in the hotel's kitchen, pushing housekeeping carts, and delivering luggage to guest rooms. As a result of his experience, Tisch made immediate changes within the company, including ordering new uniforms for staff. In addition, Tisch instituted a new program for Loews's senior management team, through which managers make a short rotation into a different department each year. At the end of the rotation, the senior manager conducts a roundtable discussion with department employees to ferret out issues.

After a series of acquisitions, trust in senior management dropped precipitously within a large multinational business unit at Cargill. Mistrust at this agribusiness giant was so serious that it carried over to the business unit's new senior management team. To turn this situation around, the business unit's entire senior management team traveled to each of the unit's locations—including six international locations—to meet face-to-face with employees in small groups and ask the employees what the senior managers could do for them. As a result of this and other actions, employee trust in the senior management team doubled in just eighteen months. According to Cargill organizational effectiveness consultant Sarah Strehl, "They really just put their money where their mouth was. They committed to things and then went and actually did them. That sent a powerful message."

> You can't cut costs when you're sitting there driving your leased Mercedes from your palatial home. You've got to come back down to reality and become part of the troops.
>
> —DAVID FERRARI, PRESIDENT, ARGUS MANAGEMENT

 Keith Whann, CEO and general counsel of Columbus Fair Auto Auction of Columbus, Ohio, has found that one of the best ways to solicit employee ideas is to have lunch with them. Therefore, several times a year Whann and his executive team invite the company's 700 employees to set their work aside for a couple of hours and join them for lunch—and to voice any ideas they might have to improve the way things work. Says Whann, "We've had some of our best ideas come from employees who say, 'Why do we do it this way?' 'Because we've always done it this way.' 'Because it would work better if you did it this way.'" Employee ideas have helped the company grow to $38.5 million in annual revenues.

After losing more than $2 billion in its US operations in a recent year, new Mitsubishi North America chief executive Hiroshi Harunari believed that one of the first things he needed to do to turn around the company's fortunes was to win back the trust of its dealers. Within his first two months on the job, Harunari personally visited 139 different Mitsubishi dealerships in twenty-nine states with the goal of listening to dealers' concerns. In the year after his arrival, US automobile sales increased 8 percent, and Mitsubishi made a $5 million profit on the operation. Says Hiroshi Harunari, "Visiting a dealer's place of business is like visiting their home." It shows "we appreciate them." Says Mike Graeber, who owns a Mitsubishi dealership in San Bernardino, California, "We finally feel like our voices and concerns are going to senior management."

After being promoted into a position leading the BT network (formerly British Telecom) planning function, a senior manager invited two members of his team—one a manager, and one a front-line worker—to videotape a three-minute interview with him where they are to ask just one question: "What's on your mind, Bob?" The senior manager then says what's topmost on his mind. The video is then distributed to the rest of the organization's employees via regular team meetings, with an open invitation for them to comment via a dedicated space on the company's intranet. The video was so successful that it has become a monthly event. Says Andrea Wyatt-Budd, leader of engagement and internal communication at BT Wholesale:

His sense at the moment is that, from the emails that he gets, he has a much more committed organization. People are having more honest conversations. They're not just telling him good news. And they are getting to grips with his vision and direction much more readily.

At *Fortune* 500 automobile parts manufacturer Tenneco of Lake Forest, Illinois, a lack of trust—driven in part by high turnover in the top-management ranks—was causing rampant employee dissatisfaction. This situation was turned around when Tenneco's top-management team began to speak frankly with line employees, rebuilding the bridges of trust. As a result of this initiative, more than 80 percent of the company's employees believe the company is on the right track.

> We try very consciously to eliminate any differentiation between management and everybody else. That's the reason we don't have any assigned parking places, no executive dining rooms. Everybody wears the same colored hard hat. Green is the color you wear. No gold hats for the president.
>
> —KEN IVERSON, CEO, NUCOR

> The founder of a business gets to a point where his or her personal growth is much more involved with allowing others in the company to grow so that they can give meaning to their own lives.
>
> —PAUL HAWKEN, CEO, SMITH & HAWKEN

Kim Ki-myung, former CEO of Nasan Group, a fabric manufacturer in Seoul, Korea (the company has since been renamed In The F Company), made a point of learning employee names and then using them when speaking with the individuals. In an interview with the *Korea Herald,* Kim said:

I know around 250 of the company's 391 employees by name, and I make sure I call them by their names at every opportunity. I think that helps uplift an employee's spirit, and helps them perform better.

Nick Read, CEO of the Asia-Pacific and Middle East region of mobile telecommunications manufacturer and service provider Vodafone Group of Newbury, United Kingdom, sends a personal video update message to his 10,000-plus employees in more than 350 stores and offices each month. The employees can view or listen to the message on their mobile phones or on their computers via the company intranet.

Automobile manufacturer Chrysler has instituted For Our Information sessions to help connect frontline employees with the company's senior leadership team. These sessions, which usually last an hour, are held monthly and put different members of the company's executive committee together with a cross-section of about sixty employees from throughout the organization. Each session opens with a five-minute briefing by the company officer—the latest company news, what's on his mind, and what's got him worried. The balance of the meeting is devoted to a frank question-and-answer session.

At Sun Microsystems, the manufacturer of computer network servers, workstations, and storage systems in Santa Clara, California, the company's chairman, Scott McNealy, used a special forum (WSUN) on Sun's intranet to solicit employee opinions and feedback and to maintain an ongoing discussion with employees on the topics of corporate goals and direction. President and CEO Jonathan Schwartz uses his personal blog to engage employees on the company's technology directions. Business unit heads and executive vice presidents are each tasked with holding six town hall–style meetings with their employees each year, wherever they may be located around the globe. By reaching out in these and other ways, Sun's top management team helps build passion and excitement among employees and their families.

To help employees feel more connected with the company's top-management team, General Motors vice chairman Bob Lutz started the *FastLane Blog,* a place for him to post his thoughts about the company, its products, and employees. Says GM's director of communication research Kathy Collins, "It's a way for an employee on the shop floor on the other side of the world to feel connected to our leadership on a more personal level."

John Featherman, chairman and CEO of First Chester County Corp. and First National Bank of Chester County in West Chester, Pennsylvania, sponsors a Chairman's Birthday Breakfast each month at a local country club. It is an informal venue for him to engage employees where they talk about work as well as how each person is doing personally. A result: Annual revenues increased to more than $68 million.

At Northern Kentucky University (NKU) in Highland Heights, Kentucky, president James Votruba makes a point of personally meeting each and every employee soon after they are hired. According to Votruba, he tells the new employees that he and the university are "devoted to advancing the dreams of both our campus and our community." He goes on to say, "I quickly add that I know that they have dreams as well and that I hope that NKU can support their dreams whatever they may be." No doubt James Votruba's proactive approach helped the school earn recognition recently as a Best Place to Work Award winner for Greater Cincinnati. Said one employee of the university, "NKU is truly an exceptional organization with engaged leaders trying to do things right while focusing on the right things to do."

> If I were going to give advice to a new CEO, I'd just say there is no substitute for the best team, so do what it takes to get one.
>
> —KEVIN SHARER, CEO, AMGEN

General Motors (GM), one of the world's bestselling automobile manufacturers, headquartered in Detroit, Michigan, integrates its senior leadership team into the creation of an engagement culture by way of its Go Fast program. Based on General Electric's Work-Out model, the Go Fast program encourages employees at multiple levels of the organization to engage in small group discussions to solve problems, reduce redundancy, eliminate waste, and streamline decision-making. Every GM executive is required to sponsor at least two Go Fast sessions every year. Anyone in the organization can initiate a Go Fast session—from frontline employee to senior executive—if there is a problem that the company needs to address. Go Fast sessions generally last two days and involve ten to twelve employees. According to Kathy Collins, GM's director of communications research, Go Fast provides opportunities for problem-solving to enhance business results. It also shows workers that company leaders value and want everyone to proactively work together to develop innovative ideas.

Global chairman and CEO James Turley of tax and accounting firm Ernst & Young encourages employees to take their vacations by sending an annual voicemail message to them. In this message, Turley outlines his family's vacation plans for the coming summer, and he emphasizes the importance of taking vacations.

Paul Spiegelman, CEO of Dallas-based Beryl Corporation, hand-writes birthday, get-well, and congratulatory notes to his employees—sometimes as many as 300 a month! Although turnover in Beryl Corporation's industry (call centers for the health care industry) is historically high, the company has only one-fourth the industry average for turnover while being a leader in profit and growth.

The CEO at Quicken Loans sends hand-signed birthday cards to all team members and sends birthday cards and gift certificates to employees' children on their birthdays—despite the size of the increasing employee population.

During stressful times, executives at the Cigna Group, the insurance giant in Hartford, Connecticut, wheel coffee carts throughout their offices, providing welcome refreshments to employees on the front line. They find that employees often choose this form of engagement to raise and suggest solutions to current work issues.

When Herb Kelleher was CEO of Southwest Airlines, he sent copies of complimentary letters from passengers along with a personal memo to the employee involved.

> I produce the show. I think I am a strategic person. But how do I get people to grab the strategy, to get it under their skin, to get a feel for it, to get it? I can't write it in a manual. I must make a show of it. I motivate people through the show.
>
> —JAN CARLZON,
> CEO, SAS

When Nance Dicciani directed Honeywell's Specialty Materials unit, she hosted Coffee with Nance, informal meetings with employees in their offices. Dicciani used the time to briefly address business performance and encouraged people to ask questions. On a grander scale, she treated employees who were a few organizational levels below her to Skip-Level box luncheons. She inviting as many as 224 employees but not their managers. Dicciani says:

These were very well received. It put me in touch with the people in the organization in a way I could not be otherwise. But if there is follow up, you do indeed have to follow up.

Regular weekly senior leadership meetings at Microsoft begin with a segment CEO Nadella calls "Researcher of the Amazing," which highlight a success story from a work team. For example, engineers at Microsoft Turkey recently presented a new app that reads books aloud for visually impaired people. During these meetings, which sometimes last up to seven hours, Nadella often asks for employee opinions and gives encouraging feedback. The sessions clearly demonstrate Nadella's team approach for the company culture.

Former Mattel CEO Robert Eckert lunched with ten to fifteen employees in an informal roundtable to exchange ideas: Workers were chosen by HR to be a cross-section of levels and departments and all employees were encouraged to email Eckert with their ideas.

Tony Ling, vice president of HR at Internet portal Dianping, China's largest restaurant review website, describes a program to retain technical talent: "Zhang Tao [CEO] and I dedicate a lot of time to spend with staff. If you join Dianping, you will meet both of us within three months of joining. In addition, we are cognizant of the three-year itch," he says, highlighting the common occurrence of employees leaving a company three years after their hire dates. Ling and Tao personally reconnect with employees at luncheons, where employees ask questions or raise issues on any matter. Ling finds that people typically ask about company strategy, health, compensation, and personal development—factors directly related to engagement and turnover. The meeting gives leaders a chance to remind people about their personal connection to Dianping's mission and strategy, and why the work relationship matters to them.

> Once people trust management, know they're responsible, and are given the training, it's astonishing what they can do for customers and, ultimately, for the stakeholders.
>
> —JAMES HENDERSON, CEO, CUMMINS ENGINE COMPANY

Captain Michael Abrashoff, commander of the *USS Benfold,* a carrier with one of the lowest levels of re-enlistment in the Navy, was charged with turning around the morale of the crew. Captain Abrashoff wanted to do away with the perception of special privileges onboard his ship. On his first day, as he stood in the long buffet line for his lunch, one of his officers walked over to him and pointed out that as captain, he was eligible to wait in the much shorter line for officers (clearly visible to all). Abrashoff said, "No thank you, I'll wait in this line with everyone else." After a few uncomfortable minutes, those in the "officer line" began to leave their privileged position and join the longer buffet line. This powerful metaphor helped Abrashoff break down class barriers.

Once when ENSR International Corporation CEO Bob Weber was traveling with a more junior member of the team, at the hotel he was told that he was eligible for a suite. He declined, saying he didn't need one, but asked the hotel clerk to give it to the most junior team member traveling with him. The story took on a life of its own back at the office in Chelmsford, Massachusetts.

Emily Weiss, founder of Glossier, the New York–based beauty and skincare company, met a recent college graduate who was looking for a job. "Come on in and interview," she said, and the woman became her assistant. A year later, the woman wanted to work in product development. "She's twenty-two and never worked in product development," says Weiss, "but off she went to product development and helped to develop four of our best-selling products. That's the nature of building an inclusive company. When you listen to everyone, you'll find they all have something valuable to say."

> The leader needs to be in touch with the employees and to communicate with them on a daily basis.
>
> —DONALD PETERSEN,
> FORMER PRESIDENT
> AND CEO,
> FORD MOTOR COMPANY

When Malden Mills in Lowell, Massachusetts, burned to the ground, the smart decision would have been to take the $300 million in insurance and retire. Owner Aaron Feuerstein was in his seventies, and other textile manufacturers in the area were leaving New England. But Feuerstein pledged to rebuild the plant and keep all employees on the payroll during reconstruction. A few years later, employees repaid him when the company's performance was suffering. They agreed to avoid overtime work and took a cut in pay.

Danny Wegman, the CEO of Wegmans Food Markets, has chartered jets to fly all new full-timers to Rochester, New York, for a face-to-face welcome and introduction to the company's headquarters staff.

An employee at analytics software company SAS in India had a very supportive interaction with a member of upper management. When he attended the company's annual party, the managing director approached him. The employee said he was afraid, at first, because he had not achieved his objectives. The director told him he valued his work, and reassured him that the company appreciates and invests in people.

Brad Smith, CEO of Intuit, believes in transparency. He posts the unedited version of the board of director's annual review of his performance on the external wall of his office. He also posts a profile of his personality preferences, feedback from other executives, and data on how he uses his time. Because the majority of the company's 8,200 employees will not ever come near his office, Smith sends all the information to each employee—every year. During tax season, he devotes time to answer customer calls alongside frontline employees.

When former MGM Grand president Gamal Aziz joined the company, he held open-ended, face-to-face meetings with small groups of workers. Aziz recalls, "I would sit with a combination of people from different departments, and we would have breakfast and talk about whatever was on their minds."

> My role is about unleashing what people already have inside them that is maybe suppressed in most work environments.
>
> —Tony Hsieh,
> CEO, Zappos

At North Shore–Long Island Health Systems, CEO Michael Dowling speaks for ninety minutes with newly hired employees who assemble for orientation every Monday at 7:30 a.m. Dowling and members of his executive team also teach employee classes, and Dowling himself leads management instruction.

Campbell Soup's former CEO Doug Conant was known for writing personal notes and pinning them on employees' bulletin boards. He explains, "If I were just sending emails, it would feel gratuitous and automatic. In every note I try to recognize a specific thing." He ended each day by writing twenty notes to employees and partners. He estimates that he wrote 30,000 notes in his time at Campbell's.

Conant describes himself as a perennial "student of wisdom." He routinely scours leadership articles for insight into how he might "be just a little bit better tomorrow." Hundreds of management and leadership books fill his office shelves, making the point that here is a chief executive who values learning.

John Chambers, president and CEO of Cisco Systems, communicates what's on his mind to all employees via a video blog every quarter. This communication is paired with We Are Cisco, a tool that links all Cisco employees and encourages general interest stories, holiday photos, and so on. It is not unusual for John himself to chime in on a particular subject of interest.

When Paul Levy, CEO of Boston's Beth Israel Deaconess Medical Center, decided to communicate with employees through a blog, his advisors told him not to do it. "What if you have to go back on something you've said?" they asked. "Is it wise to give competitors access to information?" Levy responded, "Any organization that is not leveraging such networks is missing an opportunity." He has managed to speak to a significant cross-section of his staff in a forum that they have come to love.

Jerry Lenz, general manager of Lenz Entertainment Group recalls the incredible team and energy he experienced working with K-Tel International. The company was in twenty-eight countries throughout the world. During the 1970s and 1980s, they did $200 million in annual revenues, mainly selling music products (LPs, 8-tracks, cassettes, CDs) to retailers such as Sears, Target, Musicland, Woolworths, and so on. Lenz says:

[Company founder] Philip Kieves and his top executives knew everybody and related to everyone on a one-on-one basis. Philip would travel from our Winnipeg office to all company locations and made a point of meeting every new US employee one-on-one. Employees felt empowered because the executives listened to them and asked for input. Instead of hiring limos, our executives were picked up at the airport in a company van, and our driver gave the executives input openly and freely; there was no judging. Great ideas and needed changes can come from anywhere within an organization, and they did at K-Tel. It was like that with Sam Walton, jumping in a semi with the Walmart driver and asking for input—exactly the same street-smart kind of operation. We all had buddies in different departments and there were no dividing lines. Warehouse workers and executives, shoulder to shoulder, day in and day out.

How companies treat employees says worlds about the quality of their management. And quality management usually translates into companies with a long and successful financial story. Whether it is demonstrated through superior benefits, family-friendly policies, safety records, or union relations, a strong record on employee relations is generally an indication of forward-thinking executives thinking creatively about running a business.

—Steven Lydenbery,
research director,
Kinder, Lydenberg, Domini & Co.

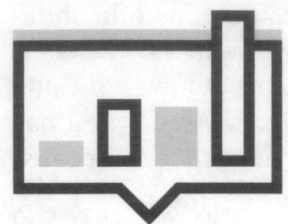

CASE STUDY: TWO GREAT SENIOR MOMENTS

Amy Esry, human resources consultant for Hausmann-Johnson Insurance in Madison, Wisconsin, reports:

My organization is really good when it comes to senior management's relationship with employees. I have two examples, one involves lunches with company executives and one involves community service.

One-to-One Lunch with an Executive

Members of the executive management team take each employee out to lunch, one-on-one, every year. So every year, each employee has one-on-one time with an executive and an opportunity to talk about what is going well, what they'd like to see changed, and to share their career aspirations. Some great feedback and ideas come from these lunches.

We have six people on our executive management team. Each executive will go to lunch, one at a time, with about nine or ten employees. Each executive has nine or ten lunch appointments to make. So pretty much every employee gets to have a one-on-one lunch with an executive each year. We usually do these through the summer. And every year we change the lineup of who is seeing whom, so hopefully, each employee gets to have lunch with a different executive every year. We provide everyone with a list of five or so questions, so employees can prepare, and all of the executives are asking the same thing. We ask what is going well at work and what needs to be improved, and this past year, we asked about recognition and communication. We change the questions a bit each year based on what we think we need to work on or get more insights about as an organization.

Depending upon what an executive hears in any particular lunch, he or she may follow up with HR or a supervisor. The executive management team meets a few times in the summer to share their notes so we can spot trends (if a lot of employees are talking about a particular issue). The executives hold each other accountable because they share the feedback as a group.

Community Service

Every year, we form teams to do United Way Day of Caring projects. We purposefully mix up the teams, so people are working with people from other departments and various levels. So it is very common to see an executive/owner digging in the dirt (literally) side-by-side with a new hire who may be very early in their career. The projects are varied: We've built playgrounds and dog gardens, done yard work for the Humane Society grounds, cleared a hiking trail, cleaned up a garden for an elderly person, helped build a garden at a school, cleaned the interior of a hospice center and at a local domestic abuse shelter, organized clothing and supplies for a local job readiness fair, to name just a few. Teams are usually made up of four to eight people. Most teams include an owner or executive. Projects typically take around three to four hours to complete, and we usually have several dates to choose from, so we don't have everyone out at once. We let employees go on the projects as paid work time. We usually have close to half the company participate in a project. Community service is very important to us, and we have a volunteer coordinator (our marketing person) that helps find opportunities for employees to volunteer throughout the year. As a result of these activities, there is no sense of management versus staff at Hausmann-Johnson. It's just people getting the job done, at work, or on a community project. There is a sense of family and team that transcends title and level. It's how people are treated on a daily basis.

OPEN AND EFFECTIVE COMMUNICATION

Most companies have an open-door policy in which any employee can approach their manager to discuss a problem. In theory, this works well; in practice it's another matter. Their doors may be open, but their minds are often closed.

In today's dynamic, fast-paced workforce, enlightened companies recognize that employees want an environment that encourages a constant dialogue between employer and employee. In my research on top employee motivators, the highest-ranking variable that 95 percent of employees want most from their managers is direct, open, and honest communication. In addition, 92 percent of employees want to be asked for their opinions or ideas, and 89 percent of employees want to be involved in decision-making where they work—especially regarding decisions that directly affect their job responsibilities.

People want to know the necessary information to do the work they're assigned, what their coworkers are doing, and how the organization is doing as well. To keep your workforce engaged, it's important to communicate information to employees about the organization's mission and purpose, its products and services, its strategies for success in the marketplace, and even what's going on with the competition. Fundamental information about the organization's policies is important for employees to understand, yet only 68 percent of employees believe their organization's policies are clearly communicated.

Feedback sessions, departmental meetings, or company-wide gatherings should ideally serve two purposes: to provide information and to gather feedback. When discussing major issues like organizational changes, always host a dialogue rather than a lecture, and encourage questions. And if any key updates are going to be shared publicly outside of the organization (for example, in a press release), make sure you tell your employees first and invite their feedback. Your employees have to feel as though they have the freedom to express their questions and concerns, and receive honest and informative responses in return.

Communication is critical to making employees feel valued, both by informing them about things going on in the organization as well as getting input from them about how things could be improved. Doing so allows employees to know they have the ability to influence decisions and be heard, making it easier for them to feel truly engaged.

This chapter will feature a multitude of related examples and strategies for keeping communication open with employees.

> I produce the show. I think I am a strategic person. But how do I get people to grab the strategy, to get it under their skin, to get a feel for it, to get it? I can't write it in a manual. I must make a show of it. I motivate people through the show. Communication.
>
> —JAN CARLZON, CEO, SAS

SquareSpace, a website-development platform firm based in New York, prides itself on open communication between staff and executives. According to the firm's CEO, Anthony Casalena, "You have to do a lot of work to communicate what we're going for, what 'good' looks like, what 'bad' looks like, what the values look like." The company is dedicated to ensuring all employees have a say and keeping the quality of their culture as it grows, which they feel they can do by keeping layers of management to a minimum. Says Casalena, "The challenge is to get all 500 employees on the same page in terms of thinking and believing. That's why the culture focuses so heavily on communication."

Employees at Intel in Santa Clara, California, use a wiki that resides on the company's computer servers to collaborate together on projects and to keep notes from meetings. The wiki has been edited more than 100,000 times and has been viewed by employees more than 27 million times.

Joe Farrell, manager of McKesson's Carol Stream, Illinois, distribution center implemented Focus Meetings for members of the facility's warehouse, office, and management teams to meet biweekly. They discuss issues and improve communication up, down, and across the organization.

Herbert Construction Company in Metro Atlanta used to have weekly meetings that only foremen and crew leaders would attend. These people managed groups of three to seven laborers. Company president Doug Herbert says:

> Feedback is the
> breakfast of champions.
>
> —RICK TATE,
> CONSULTANT

After we realized that company infor- mation and safety messages discussed in those meetings was not communicat- ed to our laborers, we changed our ap- proach. Now we have a short weekly meeting that includes every foreman and laborer in our company. Morale has im- proved, and laborers feel involved be- cause they receive the information directly and can ask questions or make comments.

Johnson County Government seated in Olathe, Kansas, encourages their employees to share goals, priorities, and learning and develop- ment interests with each other. "This information, such as the Pillars of Performance One Sheet, is displayed throughout county buildings from common areas to conference rooms," writes Teri Northcraft, human resources senior partner. The government shares results from their Citizen Survey—gauging resident satisfaction—with their em- ployees as well as the general public. They also share budget and financial information on how tax dollars are spent, other survey re- sults, and their annual report.

Every two weeks at Screwfix, a UK-based hardware company, em- ployees can give feedback to managers on any topic or issue. The implementation of a new customer card was an outcome of one of these sessions.

Employees at CustomInk, an online retailer in Fairfax, Virginia, use an internal real-time messaging system called The Circuit to improve communication. They can send feedback for any issue that arises.

In the spirit of transparency and trust, Netflix encourages employees to interview at other companies and to talk to their managers about what they learned during the experience. Patty McCord, former chief talent officer has found this practice can help employees learn how much they're worth, clarify professional goals, expand their network, and can help employees find people to recruit to the company.

New York City–based Investopedia, an online source for financial information and education, has a monthly book club to spread best practices and build relationships across functions. They have been named Best Publisher to Work for by the Business Intelligence Group for two years in a row.

Every morning at incentive company Achievers, each of the company's employees attend a nine-minute meeting called To the Point. Employees discuss the progress their departments have made and make a personal commitment to their coworkers about what they will focus their energies on that day. Employees are energized and excited after attending the meetings, and the amount of email among employees has been reduced by half.

On their first day of work, employees at Piscines Ideales—a swimming pool designer, builder, and maintenance company based in Pefki, Greece—are given the mobile phone numbers of the company's CEO and managers.

To help maintain a small-company culture at Belgian shoe retailer Schoenen Torfs, each store is assigned a coach to facilitate communication between workers and managers. These coaches solicited employee opinions when the company was deciding whether or not to sell children's shoes.

> I'm a strong believer in the philosophy that the more employees know, the more valuable they are to the company.
>
> —GAIL HERING, CEO, ATMOSPHERE PROCESSING

PepsiCo, the beverage conglomerate based in Purchase, New York, knows the value of responding to survey data. Results from a global survey showed employee satisfaction scores were highest at locations where employees said that results were shared and followed up (78 percent). Satisfaction scores were lowest at locations where employees reported that results were not followed up (51 percent). For one division, there was a link between following up on survey results to bottom-line performance. Sites where the majority said there was follow up had lower turnover, fewer safety issues, and fewer lost days due to accidents.

According to Tony Sablo, senior vice president of HR at the National Geographic Society, the organization uses broad communications practices to improve its culture. The intranet, NG Connect, was completed overhauled to be more personal. To improve the site's user-friendliness, the director of internal communications collaborates with a staff-led advisory council. The site hosts videos recognizing employees' achievements, both internal and external to the Society. The  CEO writes his own blog and facilitates informal weekly coffee meetings with up to thirty employees at a time.

Circle, a social enterprise delivering health care through a number of centers in the United Kingdom, established a communications working group to find more effective ways to communicate with the workforce during a change initiative. When it was found that many employees did not have computer access to read emails from managers, they set up bulletin boards throughout the facility. The system supports upward communication from employees, who are given wide latitude to lead change efforts. Employees report feeling valued and seeing that their contributions count.

After former CEO Dave Cote of Honeywell held an electronic town hall–style meeting each quarter to review the company's performance and goals, Honeywell surveyed employees to check their understanding and concerns for the company's future. Cote believed that "people are the ultimate differentiator."

IBM held a three-day electronic brainstorming session to develop ideas that would move the company forward. Employees generated 37,000 comments, which are now being prioritized according to greatest market and social impact by employees at all levels. IBM has turned the concept into an ongoing program to collect ideas from all employees, the ThinkPlace program.

Every quarter, Taj Hotels in Mumbai, India, evaluates midlevel managers, not just by their bosses or peers, but also by their immediate subordinates. Employees receive feedback and counseling to overcome flaws and sharpen skills.

Jack Welsh's Six Rules

1. Face reality as it is, not as it was or as you wish it were.

2. Be candid with everyone.

3. Don't manage, lead.

4. Change before you have to.

5. If you don't have a competitive advantage, don't compete.

6. Control your own destiny, or someone else will.

Steve Yi, cofounder and CEO of software company MediaAlpha, says:

We schedule videoconference meetings longer than they need to be to recreate the informal discussion that you would have in the office. We're okay having our meetings run 30 to 40 percent longer to foster closer relationships.

> If you can run the company a bit more collaboratively, you get a better result because you have more bandwidth and checking and balancing going on.
>
> —LARRY PAGE, CEO, GOOGLE

Julie Heneghan, founder and CEO of human resources firm The Steely Group, has good ideas to enhance employee engagement: Assign new hires a work buddy and/or a mentor. Ask the buddy/mentor to check on the new hire often. Match the physical setup of the employee's home office to the company's work environment. This also includes company-logoed clothing and office items.

At 3M, senior vice president of human resources Angela Lalor reports:

Leaders share priorities and expose as many people as possible to the planning process by holding frequent employee meetings and through both systematic written communications, including personal emails from the CEO to the entire employee population, their internal website, leadership classes, and in employee orientation.

One highly successful use of new technological avenues for communication comes from Deloitte, which has moved away from company-produced videos toward user-generated content. With its own YouTube channel showing staff-produced two-minute videos, Deloitte has an opportunity to glimpse into how employees view their place of work and allow management to learn from the insights and experiences of those in the trenches.

At Wynn and Encore Resorts, 1,300 supervisors were retrained to learn how to evoke a story. According to Steve Wynn, short, daily meetings before their shift starts include asking supervisors:

Who can tell us about something that happened yesterday with a guest? The supervisor calls a storytelling hotline. We then put the story on the in-house internet and plaster it on the walls. We make the storyteller a hero and do this hundreds of times a week.

To Better Communicate with Individuals:

✪ Ask employees for their input and ideas.

✪ Engage in periodic one-on-one meetings with each employee.

✪ Ask them what you could do to be a better manager.

✪ Offer personal support and reassurances, especially for your most valued employees.

✪ Provide specific feedback as to what they are doing well.

✪ Provide open-door accessibility to management.

✪ Discuss and have a development plan for each employee.

✪ Invite employees to write anonymous letters to top management about their concerns.

Serco, a UK-based service company, knows the strong correlation between customer satisfaction and employee engagement. When they reorganized internally, company executives clearly communicated the rationale for the change via an advertising campaign that included face-to-face communications, internal magazines, and posters. Employees were asked for their input during the face-to-face meetings. An employee engagement survey, which included items to identify areas to improve, was also administered. The results: greater role clarity and improved commitment to the vision and mission. Employee engagement increased along with a 12-percent increase in customer satisfaction. Substantial business growth occurred over the subsequent three years.

Pinnacle PSG, a manager of social housing complexes in Essex, United Kingdom, underwent a reorganization during which the company used regular team meetings and two-way exchanges between management and employees. They found that employees were much more prepared to move away from the old way of doing things to try new methods. Previously, employees had cleaned streets as part of one large team every month. The organization was restructured into smaller teams, each having a defined area to cover. The result: Cleaning frequency increased from once per month to every twelve days. The quality of the cleaning improved, as did overall employee engagement.

Kier Group, a leading construction, development, and services group in the United Kingdom, asked 1,200 newly transferred employees to develop icons that depicted different aspects of their ideal organizational culture. Icons represented, among others, "Can-Do Attitude," "Inspiring Leadership," "Us and Them," and "Poor Communication." Employees responded to quarterly surveys about business performance and the desired changes, and improvement groups were set up to follow up on employees' responses. The result: Employee engagement scores improved to almost 90 percent.

Diane Marinacci, director of customer service for Public Buildings Service, Region Two, General Services Administration, says her group has achieved phenomenally high scores on the Gallup Q12 survey, going from 47 percent to 75 percent, due to "the table." When employees in Marinacci's division come to work each day, they meet at a round table to talk about caseloads, share best practices, and offer each other support. Then they go to their individual work stations. Marinacci says, "More work is done at that round table than could ever happen in a cubicle. I tell my friends, if you're a boss, you need to get a round table."

> According to Melcrum, the top 5 actions a leader can take to foster engagement are:
>
> 1. 70% Communicate a clear vision of the future.
>
> 2. 46% Build trust in the organization.
>
> 3. 40% Involve employees in decisions.
>
> 4. 39% Demonstrate commitment to values.
>
> 5. 33% Respond to staff feedback.

After seeing low scores for communication with management on the Gallup Survey, London-based Pinnacle PSG established regular meetings between staff and management, emphasizing a two-way exchange to gather ideas from employees.

WSFS Bank in Delaware came out of the recession stronger than before. They attribute their success to making engagement part of their daily lives. Says Peggy Eddens, chief human capital officer, "Six or seven years ago, everybody in the bank started wearing a nametag. People are much more willing to engage you in a conversation if they know your name. Nametags are conversation starters, and when conversations happen problems get solved, differences get eliminated, opportunities get pursued."

> Employees represent a valuable information resource. If you know how to tap that resource, you can't go wrong. A great way to do this is through brainstorming sessions.
>
> —ELAINE ESTERBIG BEAUBIEN, PRESIDENT, MANAGEMENT TRAINING SEMINARS

LiveOps provides virtual call centers to large corporations. To motivate call agents, the company uses gamification to help them collaborate and carry out business tasks. Agents receive points for completing training, share knowledge, coach, or network with others. Participating agents outperformed their peers by 23 percent in average call time and customer satisfaction.

Software company Buffer is based in San Francisco, California, but has employees around the world. To promote one-to-one interactions and give employees daily face time, the company instituted a daily "pair call." The setup is completely random, and all employees are expected to participate. They share what they currently work on, discuss challenges, and offer ideas for improvement.

To Better Communicate with Groups:

✪ Have a morning huddle in which each member of team reports what they are working on and if they need any help.

✪ Be open and honest in explaining the situation and challenges going forward.

✪ Host praise barrages in which each member of the team receives positive feedback from others on the team either verbally or in writing.

✪ Conduct town hall–style meetings with members of upper management.

✪ Host CEO-led breakfasts or brown-bag lunches.

✪ Maintain a twenty-four-hour news desk on the company intranet.

✪ Take questions in advance of a meeting or allow them to be written on index cards, anonymously.

✪ Record meetings and distribute the proceedings to those who are unable to attend.

✪ Provide periodic state of the union updates on the business.

✪ Set up a blog site for your CEO to provide feedback around issues of importance.

MGM Grand in Las Vegas holds a ten-minute pre-shift meeting prior to a shift change where group managers review a daily email from the internal communications office that summarizes what is happening in and around the hotel that day. MGM Grand employees report feeling very involved and better able to provide good customer service with the information in hand.

REI has created a "company campfire" social network where employees and managers are free to gather, debate, and even argue on terms. Nearly half the company's 11,000 employees have used the tool to gain a voice in issues affecting the company and their jobs.

Daily tiered huddles occur on every level at Baylor Scott & White Health in Dallas, Texas. Through these interactions, which start with frontline teams and end at the executive level, critical information ascends within a few hours. Responses and other important information descends to midlevel management and the front line on the following day.

Another medical organization that incorporates huddles into daily work processes is Harvard Vanguard Medical Associates. For example, at their Kenmore Clinic in Boston, Massachusetts, the teams meet for ten minutes to address issues in their work environment. Then the issues, improvement ideas, and metrics are posted on bulletin boards and tracked.

At New London Medical Center, leaders wanted to improve patient satisfaction scores for cleanliness, so they asked housekeeping staff for ideas. One housekeeper said they often clean rooms while the patient is away for therapy so the patient doesn't know the room was cleaned. The housekeeper designed a card to leave for the patients to inform them about cleaning taking place.

After employees complained about having too many meetings to attend, Airbnb started a tradition of videotaping all of its meetings. Footage is edited into sharable content for people who are unable to attend.

The owners of Great Harvest Bread Company encourage franchise owners to learn from one another. Franchise owners and employees visit other franchises for new ideas and are reimbursed for half the cost of their travel. The amount is subtracted from franchise fees.

Sir James Dyson of the Dyson Company in the United Kingdom recommends:

Ban memos. People live off memos and emails and don't speak to one another. The real value occurs when we meet each other at work, spark off each other, argue with each other. That's when creative things happen. Having a philosophy of disliking emails is healthy.

COWORKER SATISFACTION AND COOPERATION

A team is only as good as its accountability to each other. None of us want to displease those we work with daily.

Every organization is made up of teams of employees who each need to work together to obtain desired goals. Thus, the quality of one's coworkers and the ability of groups of employees to work well together to achieve their objectives is critical for employees to feel engaged. This requires that any working team spend time socializing and getting to know each other, which can be done informally by sharing meals together or having common off-work activities and pastimes.

Coworker relationships can be strengthened through structured team-building activities in which employees get to work together with others on activities different from their traditional job functions:

Playing a team game as part of a learning activity, being on a company sports team, or volunteering together to build a home for Habitat for Humanity would be a few examples.

A strong team has the quality of a close-knit family in which each member works to help others as needed and for the team as a whole to succeed. That feeling of cohesiveness plays an important role in having employees feel engaged where they work. This chapter will feature numerous other examples of coworker satisfaction and cooperation in practice.

> Nothing, not even the most advanced technology, is as formidable as people working together enthusiastically toward a shared goal. Whether as a nation, an army, or a corporation—people become unstoppable when they are moved by a common vision, and have the power and tools to achieve it.
>
> —UNITED TECHNOLOGIES CORPORATION BROCHURE

At Google, team members working on the same project are allowed to share an office, making it easier to communicate and share ideas.

On the last Friday of the month, a department at the Portugal office of global real estate firm Cushman Wakefield hosts a cocktail party for coworkers. Responsibility for hosting the monthly party rotates from department to department.

Johnson County Government seated in Olathe, Kansas, uses a physical bulletin board with messages for anyone who needs a positive thought for the day. They call it their Take What You Need Board. It has proven to be an inexpensive, meaningful way to share inspirational thoughts. Some people take an item for themselves and others share with another employee or client. Created at the suggestion of employees, the boards were initially created in one department and now are located in office common areas so employees, clients, and residents have access to it.

Full Beaker in Bellevue, Washington, pays for employees to have lunch every day at any restaurant of the employee's choice in the area because they feel spending time together outside the office environment allows them to build better bonds and to collaborate more efficiently. These coworker lunches help people know each other better on a personal level, and thus, they are more productive when they work together on different projects. The company becomes stronger as well when everyone knows everyone else.

"The only condition is that an employee takes one or more coworkers with them whose lunch will also be covered by the company," says Shavkat Karimov, the company's director of SEO. "Even though we only have thirty employees, it is an expensive investment, but one we feel is worth it for the bonding that occurs between employees. We've been doing it for years." They monitor the perk, and

> If you have a workforce that enjoys each other, they trust each other, they trust management, they're proud of where they work—then they're going to deliver a good product.
>
> —JEFF SMISEK, CEO, CONTINENTAL AIRLINES

when lunch receipts are unusually high, a manager brings it up in the employee's one-on-one and that behavior stops. When an individual or a team has achieved a success, the CEO takes them to lunch as well.

At marketing and branding firm Parker LePla, employees are encouraged to join their coworkers in regular afternoon field trips. While on these field trips, participants go kayaking on Lake Union, go lawn bowling, or play WhirlyBall.

When Sherre Fairbanks, now a reward and recognition coordinator for the University of Michigan Medical Center, worked in an ambulatory care clinic, the clinic came up with an activity called Walk in My Shoes for a Day. In order to promote better interaction among coworkers—and get a little taste of someone else's job—each employee was paired up with another and essentially shadowed that person for the entire day. No position was off limits; the activity included the doctors, nurses, office staff, dieticians, social workers, medical assistants, lab personnel, and so on. Employees shadowed everything from regular office visits to medical procedures being completed. The goal was for everyone to really see what it was like in a job that was not their own and to better understand what coworkers might encounter. The activity promoted positive interaction among employees as well as giving them an opportunity to experience another job that they might be interested in and enjoy. "This activity proved to be the best thing that the office completed," says Fairbanks. "From that point on, everyone looked forward to Walk in My Shoes for a Day each year."

Says Michele Moore, founder and CEO of Southwest Human Capital, in Albuquerque, New Mexico:

A gold star, an "attaboy" on the company's intranet, or small gift cards go a long way toward establishing rapport and camaraderie. The feedback I've received is that being recognized by peers can be just as powerful—if not more so—than being acknowledged by one's supervisor. I tend to like physical tokens of appreciation, as employees love to showcase these in their cubicles or on their office doors.

Midwest Retail Services, headquartered near Columbus, Ohio, is a B2B company that sells retail store shelving and displays to stores in every category from grocery to pet supply to party stores to pharmacies. They employ about fifteen people across three or four states and have outside sales reps stationed in several other states. The company is a big believer in the power of content marketing. It posts articles on their blog intended to help their retail clients increase the sale of merchandise, improve client relations and customer service, as well as educate them on the shelving and merchandising systems that Midwest Retail Services sells.

One of the ongoing articles is called "Ask the Team." A customer-focused question is chosen, such as "How can my store increase the sales of holiday candy?" or "How can I tell what brand of shelving I already have in my stores?" or "What kinds of fixtures should I include in a new Pharmacy?" Rather than writing a generic company-authored article, Midwest Retail poses the question to their team of outbound sales and inbound service representatives. Then it compiles the best responses into a team-written article that includes multiple answers and perspectives, while highlighting the individual team member's name and role in the company. This allows the company to demonstrate the collective knowledge possessed by their employees, to amplify the perceived industry authority of their sales staff, and to provide very public recognition of the employees.

The company plans to collect the best "Ask the Team" articles and publish a printed book, creating an "advice anthology" where each contributing team member is cited for their best responses. The book will be used as a promotional marketing tool that is distributed to clients and prospects, something more compelling than a standard brochure or business card.

To inspire employees to reach out to one another and promote camaraderie, New York product development agency Dom & Tom has a coworker initiative called Dom & Tom's Do Good, Be Good Award. Each month, two employees nominate two other employees for the award. Winners are announced at the monthly company-wide town hall–style meeting, receive a trophy that they keep for a month, and a $100 donation to the winner's charity of choice given in the employee's name.

At project completion celebrations, employees at Dreamworks Animation present their personal projects to peers. This encourages appreciation of non-work ideas and showcases creativity.

Employees at Motley Fool reward each other with points that are redeemed for gift cards and prizes through the YouEarnedIt platform. Team member Amy Dykstra explains, "Employees benefit from feeling appreciated for their specific work and the company benefits from viewing a newsfeed of pertinent well-wishes every day. When things are busy, seeing recognition come in that someone appreciated my contribution means the world to me and invigorates me to continue working hard."

Johnsonville Foods in Sheboygan, Wisconsin, encourages employees to learn about other parts of the company by having every employee follow another employee for a day to learn about that person's job.

CASE STUDY:
INNOVATIVE PRACTICES IN
TEAM ROLES

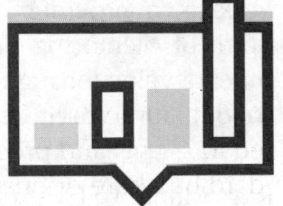

Professor David Clutterbuck of David Clutterbuck Partnership located in Maidenhead, England, shares how his employee communications company, The Item Group, pioneered a number of innovative approaches to engagement. Among them:

→ Team meetings and company meetings were led by everyone in the company (forty-five people) instead of the most senior person. Everyone took turns to chair meetings. Staff had greater control of the agenda, and it helped improve their confidence.

→ People chose their job titles. Everyone discussed with their colleagues what the core of their job was and collected ideas before deciding for themselves. Where all team members had the same job role, they decided collectively. This focused them on what was important in their jobs. We changed business cards to reflect this and of course it made for interesting discussions with curious customers and anyone they talked to about their jobs.

→ Headquarters was closed down for a day. Everyone else went out to the field to meet people they only knew as voices on the phone and to find out how they saw the world.

→ Every year, staff were rewarded with a long weekend trip overseas. Management built into the agenda half a day of work-related training, but the rest of the time was about building networks with colleagues in other parts of the company.

Sodexo, a provider of quality-of-life services in Paris, offers their Spirit of Mentoring program to encourage employees to help each other develop through collaboration, goal achievement, and problem-solving. One result: relationships that continue after the program.

Russ Mann, CEO of Covario, a designer of interactive marketing analytics software in San Diego, California, started his company's Culture Club to create opportunities for the company's employees to interact with one another. The club has sponsored a variety of events, including an online Covario Assassins game, "designed as a friendly inter-office game of 'tag' that pits colleague against colleague until there is only one survivor." Says Mann, "Client problems are getting solved faster . . . because we have more communication in the team. People feel more energized to come to work, and they're happy about the kind of work and the place."

Sabre Holdings Corporation, a travel company based in Southlake, Texas, maintains SabreTown, an online portal designed to link together the company's 9,000 employees who work in fifty-nine different countries around the globe. Similar to social networking sites Facebook and MySpace, SabreTown enables employees to create personal profiles with personal and work information, to post messages for other employees to read, to join resource groups, to ask and answer questions, to share their favorite travel destinations, and much more. The result has been the development of a global community of workers who help and support one another regardless of their particular location. One day, an employee located in Sabre's London office posted a message on SabreTown asking for advice in counting swimming laps. She quickly received seven responses to her message, including

> Think about what kind of planning environment supports teamwork. Individual spaces will be smaller. There will be more dedicated team rooms, more group spaces.
>
> —MICHAEL JOROFF, DIRECTOR OF RESEARCH, MIT SCHOOL OF ARCHITECTURE

one from Sam Gilliland, Sabre's CEO, who happened to have been a competitive swimmer. Today, about 90 percent of the company's employees are active participants in SabreTown.

Fleishman-Hillard, an international public relations firm headquartered in St. Louis, Missouri, uses a wide variety of meetings to involve employees in the business and to build camaraderie and teamwork. Regularly scheduled meetings include monthly "cork celebrations" to celebrate new business, births, and other milestones; quarterly meetings for peers within the company; and monthly meetings where company results in meeting goals are presented and discussed. At the company's Kansas City office, a survey showed that 100 percent of employees agreed that they are part of a group working effectively as a team, and that they are proud of their teams.

Alliance Castings of Alliance, Ohio, instituted a series of seminars called Value of the Person. During the course of these seminars, employees are taught to treat one another with dignity and respect while maintaining a work environment that is both safe and committed to producing high-quality products. These seminars resulted in better relationships between workers and management—and among one another—and increased teamwork and trust throughout the organization.

At Da Vita, the largest provider of dialysis services in the United States, employees vote on every decision, from logos to new business initiatives. Each of the company's 1,400 clinics has its own set of guidelines jointly developed by the local administrator and employees, known as teammates.

> A group of people working together can come up with smarter decisions than one individual, no matter who he is.
>
> —ED HOUCEK,
> VICE PRESIDENT,
> DEWAR INFORMATION
> SYSTEMS

At Boeing's aircraft manufacturing plant in Renton, Washington, management decided to dump its old production system and replace it with a new, streamlined system based on Toyota's lean production model. This new system puts trust in team members to work together to discover and solve problems on their own without waiting for management to find and fix them. After adopting this new system, the plant was able to reduce the number of 737 model aircraft in production on the shop floor from twenty-nine down to eleven. At a cost of $35 to $70 million each, this reduction in work in process has saved the company many millions of dollars.

Information technology manufacturer Cisco Systems held Kids@Work days in its Sydney, Brisbane, and Melbourne, Australia, offices. In the Sydney office, more than 150 children joined their parents at work—and enjoyed a variety of fun activities including videoconferencing, face painting, and lunch at North Sydney Oval. According to Helena Smith, group manager for human resources, "We all work extremely hard and we like to celebrate our results. An important part of that are the families. We really want employees to feel that we do consider these other important aspects of their lives and try to bring them together."

Each year at automobile manufacturer Ferrari S.p.A., ten teams of employees challenge one another with quality improvement projects for each of three four-month periods. An evaluation judges the teams' results for each period and assigns winners as follow: pole position (after the first four-month period), fastest lap (after the second four-month period), and chequered flag (after the final four-month period). One team is declared the overall winner at the end of the year-long "racing season," recognized as the occupants of the winner's platform. Says one employee, "I am proud to be part of this company, where we are all one family, part of a team of excellent people working well together."

Recruiters at Dixon Schwabl, a marketing and advertising firm located in Victor, New York, believe that assembling an eclectic group of employees helps create powerful working relationships, leading to higher levels of performance. Recruits to the Dixon Schwabl team (who are interviewed by team members during the hiring process) include a jazz radio DJ, a former professor, a bartender, a television photojournalist, and a bank executive.

Schlumberger, an oil-field-services company headquartered in Houston, Texas, has found a way to help its more than 87,000 employees, scattered in eighty countries around the world, share their knowledge with colleagues and work together more effectively. The company has organized twenty-three online Eureka communities, with areas of interest ranging from well-engineering geophysics to chemistry. These communities—along with 140 different special-interest subgroups—are self-governed by member employees, with leaders who are elected by employees to serve one-year terms.

> Not only must workers learn and be motivated to do so, managers must learn as well. Indeed, workers teaching their peers has value; nobody knows the details of a job as well as those doing it, and workers often best perceive a job's problems.
>
> —DR. MITCHELL RABKIN,
> PRESIDENT, BETH ISRAEL HOSPITAL

Defense contractor Northrop Grumman of Los Angeles, California, has installed an expertise-location software tool to analyze employee email for indications of their current interests. Results of the email analysis is added to each employee's online profile—enabling coworkers to pull together project teams of like-minded employees quickly and easily. Managers also use the enhanced profiles to assign engineers to new projects.

Hack Day—an innovation activity sponsored by online portal Yahoo! of Sunnyvale, California—teams of employees are given twenty-four hours to follow their creative instincts by creating innovative new software projects for the company. A recent Hack Day attracted 102 projects, some of which became new Yahoo! products or features in existing products. Although the employees have the opportunity to win trophies for their efforts (in categories such as Best User Experience, People's Choice, and Why Did You Wait for Hack Day?), most employees enjoy the challenge and the camaraderie of working closely with their coworkers to invent something new in a short period of time.

At beer maker Coors Brewing Company, employees in the plant logistics division in Golden, Colorado, are in charge of scheduling and setting the agenda for a monthly forum specifically designed to brief managers on issues of interest to employees that don't normally get aired in regular staff meetings. After instituting these meetings, the plant went from being one of the worst performing on its business targets to one of the best.

To become a manager at Newark, Delaware, fabric manufacturer W.L. Gore & Associates, employees must first find other employees within the company who will work for them.

Tips for Team Meetings

✪ Only invite individuals who are needed or who have something to contribute.

✪ Start on time, even if everyone isn't yet present.

✪ Have an agenda for each meeting.

✪ Ask everyone to turn off their cell phone.

✪ Assign roles and alternate for each meeting, for example, time keeper, recorder, and process monitor.

✪ Be ruthless on interruptions. Don't let team members cut off other team members. Don't allow phone calls or other outside interruptions disrupt your meetings.

✪ Be inclusive; draw out quieter participants.

✪ End on time or ask participants' permission to extend the meeting time if needed.

From an employee standpoint, a great place to work is one in which you trust the people you work for, have pride in what you do, and enjoy the people you are working with.

—ROBERT LEVERING,
A GREAT PLACE TO WORK

Beaverbrooks the Jewellers, headquartered in Lytham St. Annes, United Kingdom, recently began a program called Tell the Total Truth Faster. In this program, employees are trained how to give good feedback to one another—and to their managers—and to speak out when they are not satisfied with something about their jobs or workplace.

 Level 3 Communications, a multinational telecommunications and Internet service provider, decided on a new strategy to increase employee engagement, although employees are spread across the globe. Emily Green, talent manager for Europe, the Middle East, and Africa, incorporated Level 3's own technology to share their cultures with one another through conference calls. She also started a "learning month" during which anyone from the organization gets the chance to share something they are passionate about, whether business related or personal. Green says

It's totally voluntary it gives people the chance to practice sharing their ideas and get to see other parts of the company, which may get them thinking about their career path and where they would like to work. They see scope for lateral movement, rather than just moving upward.

To give employees unique ways to bond, Restaurant Equipment World takes employees on excursions outside of their office in Orlando, Florida. These experiences include bowling, laser tag, zip-lining, and pottery classes.

At Nucor, former CEO F. Kenneth Iverson encouraged ownership among employees, who were given the power to run the plant on their own terms. There were responsible for any problems that came up and for meeting production requirements. Teammates meet and discuss solutions to supply problems, quality issues, vacation schedules, and even disciplinary actions.

CASE STUDY:
ACTIVELY ADDRESSING
CLASH POINTS

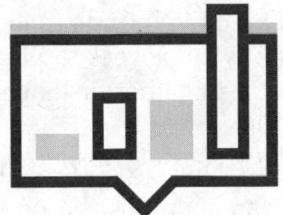

BridgeWorks, a consulting firm in Wayzata, Minnesota, helped global amusement-park company Six Flags to encourage its employees to focus on and join forces with all multigenerational members of its workforce. Six Flags wanted to address "clash points," that is, conflict when two generational perspectives meet. They specifically needed to train seasonal Generation Edgers in bridging generational divides. They implemented their customized ClashPoint training program for over 29,000 employees at thirteen parks. The program included interactive material designed to address trainees' experiences, ages, and organizational roles. The initiative began with an interactive presentation that told the story of each generation, how they started in the workforce, their defining traits and stereotypes, and their values. Six Flags dug deeper and made the training content applicable and approachable to park employees. It was designed to inspire healthy discussion and focused on loyalty, empowerment, and burnout. They used a train-the-trainer model, which included preparing a few facilitators or HR professionals to run the ClashPoint program in their own parks.

The entire sales staff at Mint Physician Staffing in Houston, Texas, works late one night a month to hunt for new business. A catered meal and cake are served to celebrate all the birthdays for that month. Those who stay may come in an hour later on the following day.

A few decades ago, Southwest Airlines captain Cliff Slaughter created the Cutting Edge program where pilots work on an airport ramp to learn what is entailed when a plane is at the gate. As a result of the program, agents and pilots had a better understanding and empathy with one another.

Dotson Iron Castings in Mankato, Minnesota, expects at least 50 percent of its employees to visit a customer, supplier, or another foundry each year to gather firsthand information and ideas for working together.

San Diego's Cidera Therapeutics drug company believes that researchers must be open to different viewpoints. To promote collaboration and teamwork, the company invites employees to attend an annual fishing trip, spa days, or golf games.

Lola, a travel startup in Boston created by Kayak cofounder Paul English, offers its staff of fifty-three a nutrition program with a built-in competition. The cost of $10,000 includes paying for the group program and sharing the cost for individual coaching 50/50 with employees. Stacey Scott, vice president of people operations, says, "The most important aspect of the offering (aside from building healthy habits) is that the staffers are getting to know people they don't necessarily work with each day.

Phil Wilhelm, general manager of people at SHI International, a software firm based in Somerset, New Jersey, reports that the company invests about $50,000 annually to offer a comprehensive fitness program that includes Mindful Monday, Camp Gladiator Tuesdays, and Yoga Thursdays, as well as two onsite traditional workout facilities. "About 100 people per week participate, but more important than getting fit is the camaraderie," says Wilhelm. "We believe that workplace friendships are a key component in retention and employee productivity."

AVAILABILITY OF RESOURCES

Make sure people have the tools to do their work!
What could be easier? Yet, most employees struggle
every day with this challenge in some way.

Once employees know what is expected of them, they need access to all information, tools, and resources to do the best job possible. This is a major challenge given only half of employees report they have the proper equipment to perform their job functions! This sounds extreme until you think about the typical challenges employees have in most any job, for example, waiting for an approval to spend resources on needed office equipment, which in turn is dependent on waiting for the budget to be finalized, which is held up because a key executive is out of the country until later this month, and so on. Or submitting a request to the IT department to make a software change that could save the company time and money, enhance customer service, or improve a work process only to learn that department is backlogged with other software projects for at least seven months. The list can go on and on.

Robert W. Johnston Jr., a clinical quality management analyst at Gateway Health in Pittsburgh, Pennsylvania, makes the case for the importance of resources:

I never knew how much my creativity had been stifled by a lack of resources until I joined my current organization. In a previous role, if I needed a report, for example, I had to submit a formal request to the Report Steering Committee, which was a group of individuals charged with determining if a report request warranted the attention of the IT team. That committee met only monthly, so if you requested a brand new report and were justified in your request, you were lucky to receive the data within six weeks (assuming they approved it).

Now, I log into a web-based portal, which has an option for submitting report requests directly to the IT Team. Once submitted, you are given a request number for tracking purposes. An analyst on the IT team fills the request, provides your data, and closes the ticket. To date, I have never waited more than seventy-two hours for a report. This includes requests with very lengthy and detailed specifications. As a result, I have completed proposals in record time, built entire dashboards from scratch, and analyzed data faster than ever. It is truly amazing what can be accomplished with access to appropriate resources.

In my research on what most motivates employees at work, "autonomy and authority" were top motivators for today's employees. All employees need to have a say in how they do their work to make it more meaningful. When employees find their work to be meaningful, they become more engaged and effective. It's critical that they go beyond their job descriptions to do whatever they can to make a difference not only in their jobs but also for the greater good of the company. Managers can encourage increased autonomy by:

→ Allowing employees to approach anyone they need for help.

→ Giving them the authority to use resources.

→ Permitting them to take the actions that are necessary to get the work done.

Once employees have been enlisted to get involved and make suggestions or improvements, they need to be encouraged to run with their ideas, take responsibility, and champion those ideas through to closure and completion. This chapter will feature numerous examples for how obstacles can be overcome so that materials, equipment, and budget can be provided to employees to do their work more effectively.

> You have to organize so people have the authority to do their jobs. But you need enough control to understand what's going on.
>
> —FRANK V. CAHOUET,
> CHAIRMAN, MELLON BANK CORPORATION

Cara Silletto, president and chief retention officer for Crescendo Strategies in reports:

Our staff are encouraged to find and suggest software we could purchase to make their work easier and faster. Each year, we implement at least one new system to gain efficiencies and streamline our processes.

Managers at Norse, a facilities management firm based in Norwich, England, know that employees who lack resources to perform their jobs will quickly become frustrated and less productive. To prevent this from occurring in their work environment, the company makes significant investments in plant equipment, personal equipment, and protective equipment.

RIVA Solutions in McLean, Virginia, provides the tools and resources for employee collaboration, such as Basecamp, an online project management platform that is designed to share priorities, brainstorm ideas, assign follow-ups, and manage information in a transparent fashion.

Stephen Howard, publisher of *Broker World Magazine,* attests to the culture of National Life Group: "National Life is doing whatever it takes on the inside to equip people at all levels with the information and resources they need to make good business decisions and offer great service." They bring in others within the insurance industry, such as brokers and adjusters, to talk to different departments so that employees can understand the business better and be of greater service to customers. National Life also designed a simple profit and loss statement to help all stakeholders make good business decisions and more fully understand what impacts the bottom line.

San Francisco–based coin exchange company Coinbase turns its cafeteria into their Crypto Club where new employees learn the basics of virtual currency.

Convercent, a compliance software company in Denver, Colorado, helps its own employees get quick answers to compliance questions using a chatbot. "When an employee opens the code," says CEO Patrick Quinlan, "a chatbot appears in the corner to ask 'Do you have a question?' Employees can report an issue, access additional resource or ask questions right then and there."

After discovering that its sales representatives spent only 30 percent of their time in their offices, the real estate department of computer networking giant Cisco Systems decided to fully support the mobility of these employees. By creating a desk-sharing arrangement for its sales representatives, the company was able to decrease its office needs while providing better support to employees. In addition, the changes saved the company $12.6 million over a recent five-year period.

Timothy Welch, a chief systems engineer for SaaS PowerDMS, was supported with the resources to travel around the world through a company program called Remote Year. He appreciated SaaS's willingness to allow him to telecommute. They also let employees lengthen their time away from the office by adding remote work options to a vacation. For example, they can go to London on holiday and add a week-long work session in Wimbledon without losing more vacation time.

> I thought, my God, if I can get people pumped up, wanting to come to work, what an edge that is! That's the whole secret to increasing productivity. I saw them push and accomplish things they never thought were possible. I saw satisfaction on a daily basis.
>
> —JACK STACK, CEO, SRC

CASE STUDY: A TEAM APPROACH TO EXCEPTIONAL QUALITY

To achieve their goal of getting a Forbes Five-Star rating for their signature restaurant, Twenty-Eight Atlantic, Wequassett Resort and Golf Club in Massachusetts developed and implemented a new employee training plan.

For prework, front-of-house employees learned everything about the menu, drinks, and the art of providing exceptional service; back-of-house workers learned everything needed to prepare high-quality food. Then Wequassett designed the workshop.

Workshop

The beginning of the workshop reviewed criteria used by Forbes to award its stars. The body of the workshop had two main parts.

In Part 1, the front-of-house group described menu items aloud, and the back-of-house group had to name the item and tell them how best to explain the dish to diners. Servers found the activity inspirational.

In Part 2, the back-of-house team prepared and presented food items to the front group.

After looking over and sampling the dishes, both groups completed an inspection form. Chefs gained an appreciation of the look and feel of dining from the customer's perspective, and needed changes were made in the kitchen.

Results

Guest service index (GSI) scores improved significantly, and after one year, Wequassett achieved its goal when Forbes awarded its Five-Star rating to Twenty-Eight Atlantic. Restaurant revenues increased with a combined 10.29 percent growth in dinner and beverage.

Black & Veatch, an engineering, procurement, and construction company based in Overland Park, Kansas, needed to implement ethics and compliance training for its 11,500 employees located at 100-plus offices and projects in over 100 countries. Because this type of training is often ineffective in other companies, Peter Loftspring, the firm's global ethics and compliance leader, aims to make ethics more visceral. Loftspring says, "I want to make people feel more uncomfortable." As *Forbes* writer Patrick Quinlin explains, "The idea is to put people in near-real scenarios in order to show how they would truly feel and react. That way, if and when it happens in real life, they'll know how to make the best choice."

A group of employees participated in the program. After they donned headsets and accessed the videos via YouTube on their phone, they experienced several compromising ethical situations firsthand. Within a two-week period after the program started, 99 percent of the participants completed it.

> We can invest all the money on Wall Street in new technologies, but we can't realize the benefits of improved productivity until companies rediscover the value of human loyalty.
>
> —FREDERICK REICHHELD, DIRECTOR, BAIN & CO.

Marsh & McLennan Companies had a huge challenge when they were planning to launch its new code of conduct. This professional services firm with 60,000 employees worldwide decided they needed to make a movie. But not just any movie. They hired award-winning director Ryan Fenson-Hood to produce a fifty-minute documentary that portrayed five employees from different cultures speaking different languages. Entitled *Faces of Marsh & McLennan,* the movie showed how these employees addressed several workplace and external challenges. Employees loved the movie, which ultimately helped meet the goal of explaining the new code of conduct across cultures.

Oppenheimer, the wealth manager and investment banking firm based in New York, launched OpcoCentral, a portal to the company's social network and e-learning curriculum. "We're committed to developing and supporting our talent at every level," says Robert Lowenthal, Oppenheimer Management Committee chairman. Opco-Central also serves as a dashboard and provides the appropriate technology to support the company's focus on communication and skill development. The site has two components: One is called OpcoUniversity is the e-learning curriculum that rounds out the firm's in-person learning workshops. Employees have immediate access to the online resources twenty-four seven from anywhere in the world. The curriculum also offers elective courses, which employees can learn at their own pace. The second component is called OpcoSocial, a social media platform that gives employees the opportunity to col-

laborate with others in real time. They can form groups to flesh out ideas with any other employee in the company. Joan Khoury, the company's chief marketing officer, says, "Technology is becoming increasingly critical for financial services organizations, and OpcoCentral empowers employees to reach the level of business agility they need to thrive."

Online grocery company Ocado uses the Slack communication app, which allows its workforce to send multimedia messages to anyone in the company. Slack's best feature is its "channels," which contain subchats dealing with specific matters. The app can also be used for small groups and teams to communicate with each other. "Slack allows people to quickly update on a conversation," says Anne Marie Neatham, the COO. Ocado's employees can establish their own Slack groups, such as Random Lunch, which pairs group members with people they never ate lunch with before. The app also helps to elevate voices. For example, a junior staff member may never raise a question during a meeting with senior management, but with the flat structure of the app, all comments in a channel are given the same weight and presence. "In just over four years it has grown to more than 9 million active weekly users," writes Madison Darbyshire of the *Financial Times,* "and 50,000 companies pay for the platform. Clients include NASA, 20th Century Fox, the US State Department—and the *Financial Times.*"

When AT&T, the telecom giant based in Dallas, Texas, replaced its outdated phones, it needed to retrain 100,000 of its 240,000 global employees. These employees filled roles that would not be necessary in the coming years. To resolve the issue, AT&T developed the Workforce 2020 initiative, which cost over $1 billion. Employees love it, and for the first time ever, AT&T made *Fortune* magazine's list of the 100 Best Companies to Work For.

Piscataway, New Jersey, heating and air conditioning manufacturer Trane assigns coaches to employees as "guidance counselors" who help them better find their way through the large organization. In one example of how the coaches work, James Freeman, an accounting team leader in the company's plumbing department, had an idea to cut Trane's cost for office lighting. No one would listen to his idea—that is, until his coach stepped in and tutored James in how to better present his case to management. The result? James's idea was approved, and Trane spent $135,000 on energy-saving light bulbs.

In his book *Getting Employees to Fall in Love With Your Company*, Jim Harris suggests four key strategies to emancipate the action of employees:

1. Allow freedom to fail and try again.

2. Create freedom from bureaucracy.

3. Encourage challenges to the status quo.

4. Give everyone input into firing the right customers.

C. Mark Seiley, vice president and managing principal of Dallas architecture firm Leo A. Daly, believes that the best way to equip his eighty-five employees for success and happiness is to give them the physical and emotional tools they need, and then stand back and let them do their jobs. According to Seiley, the physical tools include:

→ The best technology, including computers and programs.

→ A work environment that is comfortable and that encourages employees to do their best job.

And emotional tools include:

→ Motivating employees by giving them opportunities and keeping a positive attitude with them.

→ Letting them know that you're there to help them whenever they need it.

→ Giving them the freedom to do their work without constantly looking over their shoulders.

→ Allowing them the flexibility and freedom they need to generate quality ideas.

Japanese pharmaceutical company Daiichi-Sankyo of Tokyo uses videogames to train many of its salespeople. Employees role play as robots, whose task it is to kill onscreen creatures. When the salesperson shoots and kills a creature, a statement providing information about one of the company's many pharmaceutical products is displayed. According to Debra Asbury, director of primary-care sales training at Daiichi-Sankyo, "Our sales force is made up of a lot of Generation X and Yers. We wanted something that would engage our employees."

According to Mike Morrison, dean of the University of Toyota, the company "periodically takes people out of their typical office environments and let them develop ideas in places where the pressure is off and they can brainstorm without the demands of the workplace. The company also provides lots of information and reading material on the subject at hand."

When the going gets tough, some organizations are prepared to meet extraordinary needs because they have developed or cross-trained special teams. For example, when the financial markets got busy, the Charles Schwab company recruited and trained a special team they called Flex Force to help answer phone calls. The Marriott hotel chain cross-trains administrative assistants to help out as banquet servers when they have insufficient staff. Both organizations report improvements in productivity and performance, in addition to saving money.

Maimonides Medical Center in Brooklyn created a new role in the organization called engagement ambassador. To fill the roles, they selected people from a cross-section of management and union employees. Ambassadors have been an important part in explaining the concept of employee engagement to the workforce. They have also helped increase the return rate of completed employee surveys, despite the added challenges of hurdling language barriers and some employees' lack of access to computers. President and CEO Pam Brier says, "We needed to ensure the engagement ambassadors represented key employee segments. They speak the language and have the trust of their peers."

CRC Health Group's facilities are spread out across the United States, so they used a blend of online activities, virtual learning, and in-person workshops at regularly scheduled leadership meetings to build and sustain momentum while building a culture of engagement.

The online retailer Zappos encourages employees to read books from their library to help them grow both personally and professionally. Many are books that have influenced thinking at Zappos and helped them try new ways of conducting business.

To give employees the chance to learn and fail in a safe setting rather than in the kitchen, Louisville's Kentucky Fried Chicken uses virtual reality to train its employees how to cook. Walmart and Facebook also use virtual-reality training for its employees.

When a challenging or upsetting event, such as a death in the family, befalls their coworkers, employees at Accenture can donate their unused paid time off to colleagues.

In India, 70 percent of business process outsourcing companies, those providing services for companies based in the United States, were on the outskirts of the cities and the work hours were not standard. EXL Service in Noida began providing shared accommodations for its employees and also paid their water and electric bills.

Famed for their company perks, Google is serious about employee morale. Their analysis of their work culture has resulted in new policies. After learning that attrition rates for new mothers had risen sharply, the company responded by providing an enhanced parental-leave policy. This resulted in a 50 percent drop in attrition for new mothers.

Case Study:
The Pillars of Performance

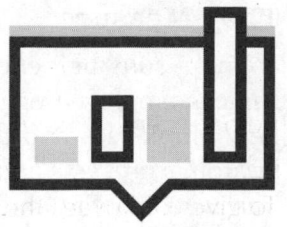

Johnson County Government engages not only their public servants but also their clients and citizens. Seated in Olathe, Kansas, the government has more than 3,800 employees serving 575,000 residents—the most populous of the state's 105 counties. The foundation of their efforts is called Pillars of Performance, which defines how they perform their everyday work to make the county a community where people want to be, work, and live. The Pillars of Performance, developed as a result of their commitment to public service and high performance, serve as the standard resource employees regularly refer to.

Teri Northcraft, the human resources senior partner, writes:

We encompass Pillars of Performance in everything we do from recruitment to performance measures—Pillars of Performance and Development—which empowers employees to share their goals, priorities, and learning and development interests with each other. This information, such as the Pillars of Performance one sheet, is displayed throughout county buildings from common areas to conference rooms.

We have a program called Leadership Empowers All People (LEAP) through which we have trained well over 3,000 Johnson County employees. We believe that the training has a positive impact on employee engagement.

Empowered Employees

Everything they do is an outcome of keeping a pulse on employee engagement. Departments are empowered to do this in ways that work for them. "To guide each individual and each department," writes Northcraft, "we created an Employee Engagement Best Practices Playbook as a result of our most recent survey in an effort toward moving the needle."

They Measure

To make sure their efforts are effective, Johnson County Government surveys employee engagement every eighteen months. They survey new employees and applicants to make improvements on the on-boarding process, and regularly survey exiting employees to track trends to identify and make improvements. "We don't look at engagement as an event; we expect the results to be sieved through and discussed throughout the year," writes Northcraft. They put tools in the hands of their managers to share departmental feedback and plan continuous improvement with their teams.

Results

Every two years, Johnson County conducts a Citizen Survey to gauge resident satisfaction. Northcraft writes:

We rate higher than the national average on most key perception indicators, with a 95 percent satisfaction rating on quality of life in Johnson County. We are proud of our successes and believe our committed and engaged staff continuously strive to serve our citizens better. We also share budget and financial information on how tax dollars are spent, communications surveys, and our annual report.

Northcraft's group also drafts an annual "Workforce Trends and Analysis Report" to share with the Board of County Commissioners and executive leadership team. The report highlights employee turnover and the importance of engagement to attract and retain employees.

Organizational Culture

Most companies claim that people are their most important asset, but unless employees are made to feel important, they'll never believe it.

An organization's culture is the glue that binds everyone together. It represents the norms, practices, and expectations for how everyone will function together. As such, it is the backdrop and foundation for everything else that occurs. As organizations develop a reputation for being a good or bad place to work, that will serve to perpetuate the perceptions of everyone within the organization as well as those outside it. Most organizations use "core" or "shared" values to communicate to everyone what the organization most stands for and the priorities for how they will work together.

For example, many organizations—especially in manufacturing industries—have a core value of "safety first," that is, a clear mandate for all employees that no matter what job they are doing, how fast they are working, or how late a project may be, the must keep safety as a priority. This value can be implemented at many levels from picking up objects that are in walkways that could be tripped on, to having emergency shut-off controls for industrial equipment and the training for when and how to use those controls.

Many other values of an organization's culture impacts how employees feel about working for the organization and hence how engaged they are at work. This can range from work-life balance priorities to how socially responsible the organization is both internally (e.g., conserving the environment by "being green") as well as externally (e.g., how they participate in and support the communities where they are based).

This chapter will share many other examples of how companies bring their organizational culture to life as active reminders to staff.

> I don't think it's possible to make a great quality product without having a great quality work environment. So it's linked—quality product, quality customer service, quality workplace, and quality of life for your employees.
>
> —YVON CHOUINARD,
> CEO, PATAGONIA

Bren Anne Public Relations and Marketing in Ontario, Canada, has five staff members who work remotely most of the time. Every morning, a positive message and a reminder of how important each and every team member is posted on Facebook and or via an email blast. Examples used include:

→ "Teamwork divides the tasks and multiples the success."

→ "Individually, we are one drop. Together, we are an ocean."

→ "That moment when you and a teammate know exactly what you're doing, without saying a word."

"It works very well for us, and every morning we hear from our team that they look for that positive reinforcement and message of positivity to get the day going," says Bren Anne.

Midwest Retail Services, headquartered near Columbus, Ohio, is a B2B company that sells retail store shelving and displays to stores in every category from grocery to pet supply to party stores to pharmacies. They employ about fifteen people across three or four states and have outside sales reps stationed in several other states. Each month the owner, Matt Ray, features a new quote at the entrance to the building. The quote is chosen by a different employee at the start of each month and shared with the team during their daily stand-up meeting. The employee reads their chosen quote, explains why they selected the quote, and how they feel it applies to them personally and the company in general. The quote is framed at the entrance to the offices where all visitors can see it, as well as every employee entering and exiting the building during the workday. Quotes are shared in the company's social media account with a shout-out naming the team member who chose the quote. At the end of the month, they get to keep the printed quote, and a new employee is selected to take a turn the next month.

Each day, employees at Cincinnati Marriott Northeast hotel in Mason, Ohio, focus on one of the Marriott Twenty Basics—a corporation-wide set of values that all employees live by—rotating them throughout the year. The Twenty Basics include such things as "I do more" and "I stay flexible." In addition to the Twenty Basics, Cincinnati Marriott Northeast employees carry pledge cards that provide them with an addition set of values. In one example—the Twenty-Ten Oath—employees are encouraged to smile and make eye contact when they are within twenty feet of a guest, and then greet the guest when they are within ten feet.

Online real estate valuation service Zillow, based in Seattle, Washington, created a Culture Committee that has successfully lobbied for a variety of employee perks, including foosball, ping pong, and air hockey tables; and free all-you-can-drink soda, juice, and milk.

> Ironically, the projects that begin small and with cultural goals often generate greater proportional financial returns than those with economic goals.
>
> —ROSABETH MOSS KANTER, *WHEN GIANTS LEARN TO DANCE*

By banning Friday meetings throughout the organization, management at San Diego, California's Scripps Health believes that employees can finish their work for the week—and then prepare for the coming week—before they leave for the weekend. Employees return to work on Mondays refreshed and recharged.

Consultants who work an average of more than fifty-five hours per week for five weeks in a row at Boston Consulting Group are placed on a Red Zone report. This report helps company managers, officers, and project leaders identify employees who may be subject to burnout, and appropriate action can be taken.

Dr. Mark L. Johnson is a university professor in the College of Technology at Pittsburg State University located in Pittsburg, Kansas, within the Department of Technology and Workforce Learning. His division within the department offers online degrees in workforce development and a master's degree in human resource development. He reports:

We are small with just four faculty members in our division, but last year we decided that we wanted to up our game and do what we do better.

The four faculty in the division all bought and read Magnetic Service *by Chip and Bilijack Bell. It's a great book about rethinking how we treat each other and our customers. We immediately began to implement ideas from the text. Instead of the department sending out a single form letter out to a prospective student interested in the program, all four of the faculty write a note of thanks for their interest to each applicant. When students come for a visit, they get to meet each of the faculty personally. We celebrate each other as colleagues more, and every week, we ask ourselves if we are providing magnetic service.*

From a personal perspective, the workplace is much more positive, and the response rate of interested students is yielding more applicants. Current students in the program have noticed the positive change and have even commented on the significance of how faculty are working with students.

Positive ideas from outside an organization are such a great help. As I tell my students, "We only know what we know until we learn something else." That something else is what makes the ordinary extraordinary!

Advanced Patient Advocacy (APA) in Richmond, Virginia, is proud of its focus on The APA Way, which represents "compassion for people and passion for results." The company helps drive this focus on a daily basis by recognizing and rewarding employees for demonstrating the organization's culture and values.

Employees self-report on a form designed to capture important details. "The customer success team shares this information with our clients to demonstrate the value APA and the staff provide them every day," says Amy Wight, director of employee success. At the end of each month, one submission is chosen that best demonstrates The APA Way, and that employee receives a $10 Starbucks gift card. This person is also recognized on the company intranet page and in the bi-monthly e-newsletter. At the end of the year, the names of everyone who submitted a form are entered into a raffle for a $50 Visa gift card.

The organizational culture is also reinforced through group activities at monthly meetings. "Activities range from a trivia challenge to understand the remaining uninsured population, to a creative exercise that allows teams to design their own 'coat of arms' to represent each APA value," adds Wight. "A guide for each activity is shared with all managers in the Managers' Toolbox on the company intranet page as a tool to use with their teams."

....

"Animals make the environment less stressy," says Alan Beck, director of the Center of the Animal-Human Bond at Purdue University. "When you talk to another person, your blood pressure goes up. When you talk to animals, it goes down." Many companies in the Maryland area use Squeals on Wheels, a traveling petting zoo based in Potomac to help employees de-stress. Discovery Communications hosts an animal petting party. Aronson accounting firm in Rockville also hires Squeals on Wheels during crunch time. Employees at Dataprise in Rockville report they feel calmer after spending time with puppies. One employee says, "I juggle multiple tasks, so it's nice to juggle multiple puppies."

Denmark-based LEGO, the famous toy manufacturer, keeps an ongoing focus on wonder and imaginative play, which thoroughly defines the company's culture. The CEO believes that values at work should match the values the company builds into its products. Instead of having traditional office structures and furnishings, they have created a physical work environment that is more conducive to play. During product testing and tours, children often visit and play with the work teams. Lego wants an environment that encourages freethinking versus having a stodgy, run-of-the-mill worksite. Thus, you won't find an employee manual anywhere on campus.

Joe Campagna, owner of My Virtual HR Director, an HR consulting firm based in Parlin, New Jersey, installed BenefitHub—a platform that gives people access to an employee discount marketplace—into three of his client companies. The platform was referred by David Flook of AdminiSMART, Eatontown, New Jersey, a national clearinghouse for HR consultants and vendors. "It's used by five of ten largest employers in the United States," says Flook. Campagna's firm put BenefitHub discount portals in a 120-employee religious organization, a thirty-employee collection firm, and a seventy-employee manufacturing company. Reports showed great results. "After six months, the average participation rate was 72 percent," says Campagna, "and 93 percent of the employees using the system returned, with 34 percent returning every month. Management loved the idea of helping their employees save money and having a great perk to set them apart from their competition."

> People want to be challenged. They want to look forward to a challenge. Money isn't everything. I want to create a culture where people look forward to coming to work in the morning and feel good at night when they leave.
>
> —BOB CANTWELL,
> PRESIDENT, HADADY CORPORATION

CASE STUDY: GROUNDING CULTURE AND MISSION DURING ONBOARDING

"Our new employee onboarding process is designed to engage our employees in the culture and the mission of KHC from the first day," says Dr. Amy Smith, deputy executive director for business services at the Kentucky Housing Corporation in Frankfort, Kentucky. "We use the process to explain our corporate strategy and how each employee supports the mission. It is branded—'KHC Unite: Where Uniting Families with Homes Begins with You.'" The process for onboarding follows:

→ A supervisor hires the employee and sets a start date, then contacts the employee via e-mail or phone one or two times prior to their start. This can include sharing job information, expectations, reading materials, and so on.

→ Employee services mails a welcome packet with important paperwork and the Employee Handbook saved to an external drive, all packaged in a KHC leather padfolio.

→ The technology services, business logistics, and employee services departments work together with the hiring supervisor to provide the needed office and desk setup, as well as the appropriate computer setup (desktop, laptop, Surface) for the employee's work (full-time onsite, part-time onsite, or remote).

→ Employee services provides a "Welcome" card to the supervisor for all coworkers in the work area/department to sign prior to the first day of work. The card is presented along with onboarding gifts, a color-matched green bag that includes the following KHC logo items: coffee mug, tumbler, mouse pad, lined writing pad, lapel pin, and ink pen. These items and a copy of KHC's Strategic Direction are placed on the new employee's desk prior to arrival.

→ Employee services also places a "Welcome" sign with the new employee's name on it on the door of the office or cube wall to alert current employees that the new hire should be welcomed into the corporation.

→ The supervisor creates and shares a thirty-sixty-ninety-day plan with the new hire. One of the most significant parts of this process is that the supervisor must commit to spending time on a regular basis, usually weekly or biweekly, reviewing that employee's work and progress in taking on tasks, adapting to the culture, and understanding KHC.

→ Finally, on the new hire's first day, they participate in a series of meetings with the employee services staff to get an overview of KHC as well as work on their new-hire paperwork. They also meet with technology services to set up their technology, business logistics to learn the phone and badge/security system, communications and marketing to understand how we communicate through staff the mission and products of KHC, and legal/internal audit to understand policies that impact employees (such as the "clean desk" policy, information security policies, and so on). The area/department coordinates a welcome lunch on the new hire's first day, and supervisors assign a mentor or a guide to provide assistance to the new hire for the first ninety days and beyond.

Many companies have added a new role in the C-suite: the chief cultural officer, who is tasked with overseeing the companies' HR, recruiting, and education teams. The CCO helps keep company traditions and best practices thriving. One such company is email-marketing firm MailChimp, based in Atlanta, Georgia.

Software firm Full Contact, based in Denver, offers employees $7,500 to take what they call a "Paid, Paid" vacation. They can go anywhere they like, but they have to actually go somewhere. The rationale is that when people are truly on vacation, they free their minds of work issues for the length of the vacation. When they return to work, they are refreshed and recommitted to help achieve company goals.

 Miami-based technology company Ultimate Software pays the entire amount of their employees' medical insurance premiums. They do the same for their dependents as well. The company also provides complimentary boot-camp classes.

Family owned In-N-Out Burger is very popular with hamburger aficionados. Employees of this California-based restaurant chain love the company as well, and not just because they get free food every day. Competitive salaries, a 401(k) plan, flexible schedules, paid vacations, and special events are just a few reasons why employees stay engaged.

To achieve production goals at apparel and promotional-gear printer CustomInk, based in Fairfax, Virginia, the company offers its employees many worksite amenities, including a comfortable dining hall and lounge, free meals and snacks, and a very casual dress code. Beth Clark, team services manager in Reno, Nevada, says, "When you print T-shirts, you should be able to wear them when you work here." All of the perks are meant to provide some of balance with employees' demanding workloads. It appears to be working. CustomInk is considered one the best-rated businesses. It has appeared on *Forbes* 100 Best Places to Work list for two consecutive years.

"We work very hard, and we expect a lot of our employees in terms of commitment to and longevity in the company," says Laura Peterson, director of learning and development in Reno. Peterson knows the company has the right culture. She is very proud that of the sixty production artists she hired, fifty continue to work for the company ten years later.

Personal development is an important component in the work culture at Round Table Companies, a storytelling firm based in Jacksonville, Florida. "We are planning on bringing our leadership team of [twelve] to the Gestalt Institute of Cleveland three times this year for intense personal development," says Corey Blake, CEO and founder. They also address identity, marital, and parenting issues. "Supporting our staff in their lives impacts their work, while deepening loyalty to the company and one other," adds Blake.

Every four to six weeks, Betabrand, a retail clothing company and crowdfunding platform based in San Francisco, California, gives its corporate frequent flyer miles to a staff person to use on free international travel.

> Our clients are the reason for our existence as a company, but to serve our clients best, we have to put our people first. People are a company's one true competitive measure.
>
> —HAL ROSENBLUTH,
> FORMER CEO,
> ROSENBLUTH INTERNATIONAL

In over thirty states in the United States, the cost of childcare exceeds the cost of college tuition and exceeds the cost of rent in some other states. This fact is not lost on some employers. Three, in particular, who see this as an opportunity to retain parents at work come to mind.

→ SAS, an analytics software company based in Cary, North Carolina, pays for onsite daycare and preschool for the children of its employees. "Knowing your children are receiving the best possible care while you're at work is a huge relief," says SAS spokesperson Shannon Heath. "Happy employees create happy customers. And more loyal employees translates to lower employee turnover: We average around 3 percent to 5 percent versus the industry average of 18 percent."

→ Fifth Third Bank, based in Cincinnati, Ohio, offers moms on the career track a free maternity concierge service.

→ Since IBM focused on the needs of working mothers in 2015, more companies are hiring breast milk shipping services, such as Milk Stork, for traveling, breastfeeding moms. Boston Scientific employees use Milk Stork's service, which costs the firm on average just under $140 per day.

....

Prezi, the presentation-software company located in San Francisco, California, and Budapest, Hungary, recognizes the value introverts bring to an organization. The CEO is an introvert and understands that some introverts need to be alone so they can focus and get their work done. The company encourages introverts to both work independently, and as fully participative teammates. Their facilities include quiet rooms, meditation rooms, and small areas to provide "brain space."

....

Instead of giving a traditionally styled employee handbook to new hires, software engineering firm Metal Toad gives them a leather-bound journal called "Toad Lore." They have found that traditional handbooks are ineffective when it comes to communicating the company's culture. Toad Lore is different: The journal contains all the cultural metaphors and dialect that turn employees into "toads." Vice president of operations Tim Winner follows six guidelines to create an artifact, totem, handbook, or journal:

1. Manage with philosophies, not policies.

2. Find a large, passionate group to support the idea.

3. Make it creative and bold.

4. Don't overthink it.

5. Add a quote from a recently onboarded employee.

6. Roll it out with fanfare.

"Your culture matters," writes Winner. "The way you communicate your culture matters even more."

Financial services firm Citigroup has three core values, known as the company's Shared Responsibilities, that guide employee behavior with colleagues, clients, and the firm. The three core values include: providing clients with superior products and services, as well as acting with the highest level of integrity; providing all Citigroup employees with opportunities to realize their full potential, as well as respect each of the organization's global employees while championing diversity; and to protect the company franchise and safeguard Citigroup's long-term interests, culture, history, and legacy.

Furniture manufacturer Herman Miller of Zeeland, Michigan, has a core value of acknowledging the strengths and differences of every employee. On the company grounds—near a small pond—stands a statue called *The Water Carrier,* which uses beams of light to project the names of Herman Miller employees with twenty or more years of service. The statue—and the Water Carrier Award, which is given to employees with twenty years of service at a special annual ceremony—symbolizes the Native American belief that every job is important to the group's survival, regardless of title or position in the hierarchy.

The Berry Company, a Yellow Pages manufacturer located in Dayton, Ohio, introduced the upside-down pyramid as its business model. Instead of putting the CEO and senior leadership team at the top point of the pyramid, the company flipped the pyramid and put the customers at the top, followed by all company staff that interacted with customers. These two groups were made the top focus of the company. At the very bottom of the inverted pyramid was the CEO, whose job it was to support the company's sales force and other employees.

> **Good treatment of workers results in similar treatment of customers.**
>
> —Todd Englander,
> *Incentive Magazine*

Outdoor clothing manufacturer Patagonia encourages employees to live the company's values. Patagonia's Environmental Internship Program encourages employees to work for the environmental nonprofit organizations of their choice for up to two months—while receiving their full pay and benefits from Patagonia. Employees can choose to do their environmental internships in the form of a sabbatical—taking time off from their regular jobs for the entire two months—or just a couple of days a week over the course of an entire year.

Automobile manufacturer Ferrari S.p.A. of Maranello, Italy, has twelve core values, which correspond to the twelve cylinder in the company's top-of-the-line race car engines. The values include:

→ Tradition and innovation.

→ Individual and team.

→ Passion and sports spirit.

→ Territoriality and internationality.

→ Ethics and profit.

→ Excellence and speed.

The company motto at New York–based global real estate firm Cushman & Wakefield is "Have fun," so at the firm's Portugal office, employees are invited to jump out of an airplane whenever they want. Doing so includes a two-day training course in parachuting, and then a day off for the jump itself. Other fun activities in keeping with the firm's motto include Department Days Out, during which groups of employees have taken field trips to a spa, gone on a tour in a Jeep, and learned how to scuba dive.

Balancing Professionals—a staffing firm in Cary, North Carolina—gives employees time off to do volunteer work in their community. According to firm partner Maryanne Perrin, "This allows employees to step away from work in order to help somewhere in the community."

Giving back to the community is a key element in the work culture of Premier Nutrition Corporation, based in Emeryville, California. "One of my favorite things about PNC is our employees' passion and efforts to bring good energy to the world," says Darcy Horn Davenport, president of PNC. "It goes beyond the four walls of the PNC office." Despite their heavy workload, employees contribute back

in the community semi-annually. The company offers several opportunities to contribute to its community. For example, the whole
company raised $6,000 for wildfire relief as a result of a bike-riding
event through California's wineries. PNC is now launching a more
robust philanthropy program, which will double the number of phil-
anthropic partners. PNC employees will vote to select two charitable
organizations to receive the funds.

At Herman Miller, the furniture manufacturer based in Zeeland,
Michigan, employees get eight paid hours annually to volunteer in
their communities. One year, the company set a goal of donating a
total of 10,000 hours of employee service. Volunteer activities vary
from building homes with Habitat for Humanity to raising funds for
cancer patients.

The boardroom at Patagonia is used to store surfboards belonging to
employees who use them while taking breaks during the course of
their workday.

Big Four accounting firm PricewaterhouseCoopers distributed a
booklet to employees entitled "Rest and Relaxation: The Value of
Time Off." An excerpt from the booklet: "Try not to call the office to
discuss business matters or check voicemail or email. You are either
on vacation or you're at work; you shouldn't try to be in two places
at one time."

At Southington, Connecticut's Yarde Metals, the company's 665 employees can work out at an on-site gym, keep their dogs in the company kennel, or snooze in the nap room. Says founder and former
president and CEO Craig Yarde, "The real issue is how we treat people. That's what defines us and that's what I hope we are known for."

Business Environment, a business services provider based in London, England, offers a variety of incentives and perks to employees to ensure they feel appreciated by their managers and are motivated to give their best every day. Some of these incentives and perks include tours of London, bowling, group meals, and a family fun day. As a result, 80 percent of Business Environment employees report feeling fully involved at work: 86 percent report that workmates care for one another, and 81 percent are excited about the future.

Google is committed to providing the complete employee package. In addition to offering great compensation—one of the best in the United States—the package includes catered meals, dry cleaning, massages, meals, and an exceptional parental leave policy. Their people analytics team analyzes employee happiness today versus how it might be in the future. They use the results of their analysis to continuously provide evolving programs that consistently match the needs and desires of their workforce.

The purveyor of web-based products and services in Mountain View, California, has a full-time concierge in its corporate headquarters to help employees take care of day-to-day tasks that distract them from their jobs. All levels of employees have access to the concierge services, which include making restaurant reservations, ordering flowers, and recommending places to dine. This perk is in addition to Wednesday and Thursday chair massages, free on-site washers and dryers, a $500 voucher for takeout food after the birth of a child, an annual all-expenses-paid ski trip, seventeen restaurants with free food, and a roving teacart.

ZAAZ, a website consultant in Seattle, Washington, gives employees free public transportation and health club memberships. It also provides random acts of kindness—items such as lottery tickets and sweets.

AFLAC Insurance Company revamped its recognition program to reinforce the company's strong sense of family, a vital part of its culture. Employee Appreciation Week is the main thrust of the program. At the beginning of the week, AFLAC invites all 4,000 employees to watch free, family-oriented films in a rented multiscreen theater. As the week commences, free breakfasts are provided, as well as raffles for prizes. Employees have the choice of bringing their families to either an amusement park, a petting zoo, or a nature facility. At week's end, employees get a gift they can share with their families.

Best Buy Company, the electronics retailer headquartered in Richfield, Minnesota, invited part-time salesman Jake Rockwell to sing a rap song to an audience of 2,000 store managers and executives from district, regional, and corporate headquarters. Not only did Jake have the time of his life—and an experience he will never forget—but he also received a standing ovation for his performance.

Companies such as Visa, SAP, Salesforce, GE Appliances, NVIDIA, Tribune Media, Slack, Instacart, and OpenTable offer their employees "at-home, physician-ordered" genetic tests to screen for mutations linked to serious diseases and illnesses.

Clothing retailer Giordano International, located in Hong Kong, China, encourages employees to organize morale-boosting activities themselves, with the company providing the necessary financial and other resources to support them. Says Giordano's human resources director Ngan Lei-tjen, "We have learned from experience that if we take the lead in such initiatives, our staff will lose their drive as soon as we stop doing so."

> 35 percent of US workers said they'd forgo a substantial pay raise in exchange for seeing their direct supervisor fired.
>
> —THE EMPLOYEE ENGAGEMENT GROUP

At Piscines Ideales, the swimming pool designer, builder, and maintenance company based in Pefki, Greece, employees who get married receive a month's salary as a bonus, and employees who have a child receive a bonus and paid time away from work. Children of employees starting a course of studies at university receive a personal computer from the company, and employees are eligible to receive no- or low-interest loans, which they can use for any reason, including buying a home. Employees also receive a substantial discount if they have the company build them a spa or pool.

> Human beings need to be recognized and rewarded for special efforts. You don't even have to give them much. What they want is tangible proof that you really care about the job they do. The reward is really just a symbol of that.
>
> —TOM CASH, FORMER SENIOR VICE PRESIDENT, AMERICAN EXPRESS

REI, the outdoor gear company, actively encourages employees to spend time outside with Yay Days—paid time off to spend outside—sizable worker discounts on its gear (30 percent), adventure trips (50 percent), and its Opt Outside campaign that closes all 151 stores on Black Friday and pays employees to pass the day in nature.

Quicken Loans gives free tickets to concerts and sporting events at Ticket Window Thursday. Every week, the CEO announces the winners over the public-address system.

SAS offers the same benefits plan to landscapers, food service workers, housekeepers, and other support staff as they do to the professional staff. As a result, the attrition rate of service employees is far less than normal.

RevZilla, based in Philadelphia, shows appreciation in a number of ways, including a week-long ZillaPalooza with games, ice cream trucks, and catered meals during meal breaks.

> Everyone works smarter when there's something in it for them.
>
> —Michael LeBoeuf, author, *The Greatest Management Principle in the World*

In 2015, Levi Strauss required its supply-chain partners to provide their own employees with wellness resources. One example is the Nazareno plant in Mexico, where management has upgraded the factor campus with a soccer field, an ATM, and better fans for worker comfort.

Dutch sciences giant DSM reinvented itself to tackle global problems like hunger and climate change. The result is an $8.8 billion company whose stock is near an all-time high. "Purpose motivates employees better than profit," says CEO Feike Sijbesma. "They are proud if they can say 'Our company is making the world cleaner, the food healthier.'"

According to public statements from Zappos:

We know there's no way we could've achieved our success as a company without our vendors' commitment and passion, so every year we like to show a little gratitude. We take over a venue such as the Hard Rock Hotel pool or Rain Nightclub at the Palms and invite all of our vendors. Between our vendors and the Zappos team, we have over three thousand people on hand. The benefits we've reaped from concentrating on building relationships with our vendors are endless. They help us plan our businesses and make sure we have enough of the right product at the right time. When inventory's scarce, they help procure inventory on hot-selling items.

CEO Fred Holzberger of Aveda Fredric's Institutes gave 400 of his associates a day off for the following year to work for a day at a charity of their choice. There was one caveat: Upon returning to AVI, they must share their charity-work experience with him. The results were dramatic. After serving others, people changed their perspectives; their outlooks improved, and they came to work more energized.

West Marine, a leading North American boating supply retailer in Watsonville, California, hires boaters to work in its stores. Customers like interacting with employees who share their passion and commitment to the boating lifestyle.

At Casper, the mail-order mattress company, employees can be found napping or holding an informal meeting on one of the premier quality beds on the showroom floor. The company also has a sprawling floor plan here employees can gather for informal meetings or lunch, which promotes more cooperative working relationships.

To attract Millennials, some companies are offering student loan repayment as a benefit, making payments through payroll deduction and matching a portion of payments employees make. Early adopters include Aetna, textbook company Chegg, and PwC.

Axis Communications has all new employees travel to the corporate headquarters in Lund, Sweden, for a few days of orientation. Employees meet their counterparts and top executives. Every January, the entire North American organization travels to one location to plan for the future. In 2017, they visited Cancun, Mexico.

To keep up the "fanatical" level of customer service at Zappos, every new hire is required to attend four weeks of training, including two weeks in the call center. CEO Tony Hsieh went through the first new hire training course, as has every employee since. Zappos offers $4,000 to any employee who wants to quit before finishing training. Hsieh says about 2 percent take him up on the offer, "a small price to pay for cultural integrity."

At ASB's call center, teams are encouraged to gather socially after work, for instance, cycling or kayaking. These team members are building relationships that extend beyond work; they build trusted friendships and make real connections with one another.

> As a key principle of our winning together culture, we encourage recognition in every aspect of our business, manifested by special awards at the store level and appropriate cash bonuses.
>
> —MIKE ULLMAN, CEO, JCPENNEY

WeWork is a popular coworking space for startups and freelancers, based in New York and serving 165 locations around the globe. The facility at headquarters features a staircase with three impressive landings along with sofas and lounges to promote synergy among WeWork teams and more than 100 other organizations renting space in the three-story building.

In its twenty-fifth anniversary year, SAS established a work life department, which provided educational, networking, and referral services to help employees choose the right college for their children and set up a retirement plan fund with contributions only from the employer. SAS estimates that they save as much as $80 million annually in recruitment and replacement costs as a result of benefits that allow the employees to eliminate hassles in their personal lives. Since the mid-1990s, SAS has offered their Generation to Generation Elder Care program with a full-time referral specialist helping employees locate nursing homes and assisted-living facilities for their aging parents.

CASE STUDY: FROM CYNICISM TO COLLABORATIVE RESULTS

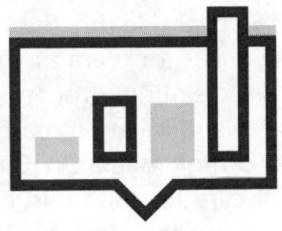

When Glenn Tunstall was chief superintendent for the Royal Borough of Kingston-up-on-Thames (London, United Kingdom), he had 450 policemen and policewomen within his span of control. His challenge was to rid his team of their cynical attitude.

Tunstall started by analyzing crime-solve rate data and engagement scores and discovered he needed to show his team that the level of employee engagement drove crime-solve rates. He replaced the usual posted data charts with a simple sign that read, "You said, we did." He wanted to reinforce the need for the team to focus on listening and acting. Tunstall also started a recognition program. Anyone in the borough could recognize others for their achievements. It became so popular that junior officers asked their managers to incorporate recognition in the their work areas.

Result

In the last few years, the Kingston police have doubled the percentage of crimes solved and reduced complaints from the community by 59 percent. Under Tunstall's leadership, Kingston became London's safest borough and achieved the highest levels of public confidence and victim satisfaction in the Metropolitan Police. Tunstall was later promoted to Borough Commander. Today, he is an Engagement Consultant. Changing the culture at Kingston borough remains a favorite achievement.

"In relation to involving staff in our decision making groups, I openly say that every great idea that we implemented at Kingston has come from outside the leadership team," says Tunstall.

WellStar Health System in Marietta, Georgia, provides concierge services for team members to take care of daily errands, oil changes, dry cleaning, grocery shopping, gift buying, and travel planning. It's free and meant to ease employee stress during the workday.

Their Back-Up Care Advantage program provides eighty hours of care for the children or elderly relative of employees so employees can feel comfortable proceeding with their workday when things don't go according to plan.

According to Bersin Talent Management Systems, engaged businesses have:

- ✪ 28% higher revenue per employee.

- ✪ 87% greater ability to hire the best people.

- ✪ 156% greater ability to develop great leaders.

- ✪ 92% greater ability to respond to economic issues.

- ✪ 114% greater ability to plan for the future.

- ✪ 28% less downsizing.

- ✪ 49% lower turnover of high-performing employees.

- ✪ 17% lower overall voluntary turnover.

When Southwest Airlines decided to modernize their uniforms, executives realized that instead of hiring an outside designer, they had great designers already on board—their employees. After communicating to the company about their intentions, hundreds of people said they wanted to help. More than forty employees met every two weeks over a nineteen-month period in Chicago and Dallas to collaborate on the redesign. Joan Mast, a flight attendant that participated in the process, called it an "unforgettable experience."

Coca-Cola hired the Gensler architecture firm to redesign the workspace for its 5,000-plus employees. The result featured a "Main Street" in the middle of its six buildings with conversation-friendly lounges, cafes, a medical center, and a pharmacy. Since the redesign, division executives choose to have more multiday meetings on campus versus renting space. Meeting costs have dropped while employee morale has improved.

FuzePlay, an educational technology company based in Salt Lake City, Utah, designs and makes hackable toys. Due to massive popularity on social media, founder Cristy Sevy created a volunteer program for parents who want to emulate FuzePlay's designs.

> Having a good time is the best motivator there is. When people feel good about a company, they produce more.
>
> —DAVE LONGABERGER, CEO, THE LONGABERGER COMPANY

At Hyatt Hotel, employees donate a lot of time to their local communities. In one year alone, more than 7,000 employees from 170 locations in forty-four countries put in 26,000 hours of volunteer time.

Office supply giant Staples has started using an online platform called Profts4Purpose to encourage employees to volunteer for the charities that are personally important to them. That's one way to encourage engagement, but Staples takes it a step further. Via the platform, employees can request that the company make a donation to their charities.

After going public, audio-products maker Skullcandy experienced a loss of the youthful, streetwise part of its culture. In response, management created a new skate environment featuring functional skate ramps and skateboard memorabilia. They focused on having a collaborative environment with incentivized performance-based flexibility.

Before Nike evolved its sustainability policy, the shoe giant asked employees for their ideas. They collaboratively came up with a new sustainability initiative hallmarked by employee commitment.

Kimpton Hotel chain is famous for the Kimpton Moment, a customer-focused strategy of providing guests with genuine, in-the-moment, exemplary service. Kimpton believes that in order for their employees to continuously provide great service to guests, the employees must experience great service from the company. They maintain a fun, informal work environment, awarding $10,000 annually to the employee who provided the best Kimpton Moment. They also have an annual Housekeeping Olympics. Managers at all levels follow an open-door policy.

....

After Hurricane Katrina, Entergy, the power company in New Orleans, Louisiana, immediately helped all 1,500 of its employees move to safer housing. They facilitated access to transportation, child care, and physical therapy. They also told employees not to worry about their jobs, that they could take the time needed to resolve their domestic problems. Terry Seamons, senior vice president of HR, says the company experienced "enhanced employee engagement and even reduced turnover."

> Engaging our employees in workplace health programs helps reduce their health risks, improves productivity, and increases employee satisfaction.
>
> —BILL RHODES,
> PRESIDENT AND CEO,
> AUTOZONE

....

Fast Company calls W.L. Gore "the world's most innovative company" because they do things vastly different than almost every other organization in the world. They have been different from their first day in business in 1958. They have no formal hierarchy, managers, job titles, or time cards. Work teams evaluate and rank the members of their team based on individual contributions, and the evaluations and rankings are made public within the work team.

....

Morning Star, a tomato processing company in Woodland, California, advocates self-management. There are no supervisors in the company. The company's mission is the boss. Each employee develops their own mission statement that aligns with the company's mission. They must convey specifically what and how that employee contributes to the mission. The policy seems to be working: Morning Star's growth rate has been in the double digits for twenty years.

Chelsea Long, a customer support specialist at Adobe Software, values the company policy that lets her simultaneously volunteer and donate money to a nonprofit organization. For every ten hours of employee volunteer time, Adobe allocates a $250 donation to the charity of that employee's choice. Thus far, Long is responsible for more than $2,000 going to charity. "You can volunteer anywhere, for anything, but Adobe also sets up many different volunteer activities, ranging from serving dinner at the Ronald McDonald House, organizing donations at Materials for the Arts, and preparing meals for the homeless at the New York City Rescue Mission," says Long.

A significant corporate social responsibility policy at the Timberland Company is its Path of Service policy, which provides all full-time employees with forty hours of paid time off for community service. When John Pazzani joined the company during tough times, he suggested to CEO Jeff Swartz that the program be discontinued. Swartz said he'd consider the suggestion after Pazzani had "done his time." Pazzani now says, "It may be a costly benefit, but we don't lose people." Timberland's voluntary turnover is in the single digits, virtually unheard of in retail. An additional benefit is that customers frequently want to sign up too.

Well known for their benefits, including an on-site Montessori daycare center, fitness gym, health center, and help with elder care and other issues, SAS keeps employees because they love their work, "creating innovative software." A systems developer who left to work for Cisco after eighteen years was back within nine months explains, "Technical procedures that took hours at Cisco typically took minutes at SAS. In three weeks at SAS I did more than I did in nine months at Cisco."

As part of Zappos's Wellness Adventures initiative, wellness coordinators randomly pull people away from their work to go and do something fun instead. It could be trampolining, laser tag, or taking a quick golf lesson.

Chick-fil-A's Wellness Center has treadmill-desk rooms where employees can sign up, take their laptop, and walk while they work.

> In research by Jim Collins and Jerry Porras, organizations driven by purpose and values outperformed comparison companies by 6 times.
>
> —THE EMPLOYEE ENGAGEMENT GROUP

For credit card company Capital One, it's not always about what's in your wallet. It's what's in bed—as in someone resting. Michelle Cleverdon, strategist for workplace solutions says, "We believe in the power of relaxation to rejuvenate and recharge, which is why we have nooks and crannies optimizing every square foot to create hideaways offering a sense of sanctuary."

Former Nucor steel company CEO F. Kenneth Iverson stopped the practice of using different-colored hard hats to distinguish functional areas. The various colors had acted as a divide among the different divisions. When workers protested, Iverson held a series of discussions with the employees to help them understand that their authority did not come from the color of their hard hats but from their leadership abilities.

Nucor has avoided layoffs for more than twenty years by adopting a no-layoff policy. It developed the Share the Pain program under which all employees take pay cuts during an economic downturn. Workers and foremen take a 20 to 25 percent cut; department heads take a 35 to 40 percent cut. The higher the management level, the higher the percentage cut. Says former CEO Dan DiMicco, "You can't build a loyal workforce that's going to give you everything they have if, when times are bad, you say we don't need you now."

CUNA Mutual Group, a Wisconsin insurer, wanted employees' opinions to shape its corporate social responsibility campaign. Through internal websites, surveys, social media, and meetings, management asked more than 900 employees to identify the kinds of volunteer work and charitable giving they found most meaningful. They found that more than 90 percent of CUNA employees cared deeply about sustainability and used this insight to develop a company-wide sustainability and conservation program.

For Sylvain Labs, a New York–based brand design consultancy, "side hustles" are part of the business. CEO Alain Sylvain says, "We celebrate side hustles. A lot of people have side projects that they're working on—we create an environment where people can be more public about it." For example, an employee who makes furniture on the side built the company's conference table.

IBM now offers employees reimbursement of up to $20,000 for expenses related to adoption or surrogacy; it previously offered $5,000 for adoptions only. According to Barbara Brickmeier, vice president of benefits, "We have a general approach of wanting to meet employees where they are." She said employees had requested the change.

Besides the on-site gyms open twenty-four seven and up to $650 in fitness credits, personal finance software titan Intuit also provides forty-five bikes for cycling commuters at its facility in San Diego, California.

> According to Gallup, only 41 percent of employees felt that they know what their company stands for and what makes its brand different from its competitors.
>
> —STATE OF THE AMERICAN WORKPLACE REPORT

Top Ways to Foster Engagement

A SilkRoad Technologies Survey identified the following ways to best foster employee engagement:

- ✪ Trust in management
- ✪ Career development
- ✪ Stimulating work environment
- ✪ Recognition and rewards
- ✪ Flexible work options (e.g., work from home)
- ✪ Learning opportunities
- ✪ Career advancement
- ✪ Salary
- ✪ Good benefits (medical, dental)
- ✪ Mentoring
- ✪ Diversified comp options (e.g., pay)
- ✪ Good pension and retirement plans

Camden Property Trust, a real estate investment firm in Houston, Texas, has a "hugging" tradition that welcomes employees and their ideas with "open arms." Perks include $20 per night vacation stays in company furnished apartments. The company also pays up to $4,500 per year for college tuition for their employees' children.

United Shore Financial Services, based in Troy, Michigan, offers employees many perks, including an on-site Starbucks, gourmet cafeteria, and convenience store. Each Thursday, the company hosts hundreds of team members at a dance party for ten to fifteen minutes, beginning at 3 P.M. The theme varies each week.

Michigan financial services company United Shore is one of the first companies to build their own in-house escape room. Designed and operated as a mortgage-related experiential learning experience, the room puts groups of six to twelve together to solve challenges, mysteries, and puzzles that each group has forty-five minutes to overcome to "escape."

Infosys offers employees an extensive slate of opportunities for reducing stress on the job, including yoga, swimming pools, aerobics, gymnasiums, and cycling. The company also hosts rock shows and festivals and various cultural activities and offers training on topics such as time management and stress reduction.

At their new corporate headquarters in San Diego, California, DPR Construction uses a giant digital dashboard to continuously tracks energy use. Employees report that they are almost 100 percent satisfied with air quality, thermal comfort, and personal workspace in the new facility, according to an independent study. Since the move, DPR has experienced a drop in absenteeism and an increase in employee loyalty.

All 27,000 employees at Cummins, maker of diesel and alternative fuel engines, are encouraged to work on social service projects in the locations where the company conducts business.

Management consultants at the Boston Consulting Group volunteer their time to a host of philanthropies such as the UN World Food Program and Save the Children. After the tragic earthquake in Haiti, the group shifted its consultants from paid client work so they could apply their expertise in disaster areas.

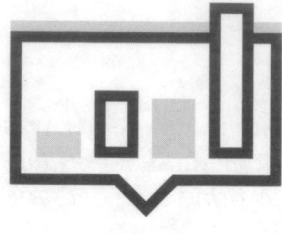

Case Study: Culture Rules Over Calculations

Antonio Rodriguez, a management consultant working in Brussels, shares an experience in which organizational culture trumped any and all rational decisions, processes, or calculations—at least until critical integration steps have been taken:

In my times as head of post-merger integration at the largest Belgian Bank, Fortis, I had a front-row seat to one of the biggest bank merger deals gone wrong. In the process, I picked up some tips on the best ways to merge two wildly different project management approaches. I also learned that nice guys finish last when it comes time to combine large transformation initiatives.

Despite my strong belief in getting the best of both worlds, I realized that if you want a merger to succeed, make it happen quickly, impose your culture, and don't allow too much discussion. People won't be happy in the short term, especially the ones being taken over, but if you can get the job done, you can rebuild your culture over the long term. Before this experience, I didn't have such a take-no-prisoners philosophy.

Working for what was then Fortis, I was part of the team behind the takeover of Dutch financial giant ABN Amro. At the time, I believed the best approach was to evaluate what each player brought to the table and to make choices based on extensive communication and brainstorming among employees. Team leaders and executive management could then select the top technologies from each company and wind up with a best-of-breed blend.

The plan called for a consortium of global financial institutions—including the Royal Bank of Scotland, Fortis, and the Spanish Banco Santander—to jointly bid on ABN Amro, then divide up the company's assets. Most mergers are decided primarily for financial objectives; there are revenue synergies and cost reductions. It's a very concrete way to show analysts and stakeholders that this is a good decision.

And in the case of this takeover, that was the case—at least on paper. Strategically it was a great decision for Fortis. ABN Amro had a global presence but wasn't doing very well, while Fortis was a strong Belgian bank looking to expand. Culturally, though, the merger was a disaster. To begin, we had Belgian, Spanish, and Scottish banks taking over a Dutch bank, that's a lot of cultures to bring together, and we were all really different. More importantly, the consortium did not operate well as a team. Each bank remained focused on its own interests instead of the broader interests of the group, which created a lot of conflicts.

As part of the high-level team conducting due diligence for the Fortis side, I spent nine months evaluating every system and project that would be impacted by the merger. We created a portfolio of 1,000 projects grouped into 130 different programs that needed to be accomplished. It was a huge undertaking, and there were at least 6,000 people involved.

We analyzed several selective criteria, including functionality, cost, and the ability to maintain the system in the future. We made our decisions based on the facts, without involving emotions. It seemed like the fair and right way to approach the merger. But the process backfired. Fortis's willingness to compromise and its desire to include ABN Amro in decision-making led to conflicts, delays, and unnecessary obstacles. On top of this, a lack of strong leadership presence in the Netherlands by the Fortis executive team made it difficult to push projects through. ABN Amro, which had a strong organizational culture, used the leadership void to impede the takeover. They took advantage of the confusion by blocking the actions we tried to take on projects.

As with most mergers, the biggest set of projects involved mapping and integrating IT systems. ABN Amro had thousands of applications. And because its team refused to share critical information, it took us thousands of hours to complete the simplest projects, such as creating links between enterprise resource planning systems. It was a frustrating experience. The lack of cooperation was compounded by the years-long integration plan. It became clear that the longer you wait to complete a merger, the more conflicts will come up. And while IT conflicts can be solved; human conflicts are tougher to tackle. You can't throw money or resources at human conflicts to make them go away. When people get frustrated, projects fall behind.

The merger failed. ABN Amro was turned over to the Dutch government, and Fortis was on the verge of bankruptcy.

Thankfully, the Belgian government bailed out Fortis, and after many discussions at the national level, sold it to the French bank BNP Paribas last year. It was very difficult mentally to go from a leadership position in a company acquiring one of the most prestigious banks in the world to failing and being taken over. In retrospect, though, I learned many tough but valuable lessons about what went wrong with the previous merger. We could have succeeded if we had taken a different approach.

A friendly merger is noble in principle, but it's also the most difficult to accomplish. If we had imposed our culture on them, it would have been more successful. BNP incorporated the Fortis team into its organizational structure and put its own people in key roles. Although the two banks have similar project management strategies relating to reporting and governance, the two methodologies diverged from a communications standpoint.

At Fortis there would have been a lot more discussion, employee involvement, and brainstorming. At BNP instead, it's a top-down approach that is more focused on speed and results. Most of the IT post-merger integration projects involved simply phasing out the Fortis systems over a set period of time and moving client accounts and data onto the BNP systems.

From a results standpoint, it was much easier and more efficient. Rather than spending months evaluating the IT systems and agreeing on a combination of technologies and tools, BNP eliminated almost all of the Fortis infrastructure. The massive undertaking was completed in less than eighteen months.

But when speed is critical, it may be the only option. There are no discussions. There are only orders to follow. It's not motivating to the Fortis team and everyone's a bit angry, but it's efficient. That efficiency enabled BNP to achieve its merger goal, and now it can focus on rebuilding what morale might have been sacrificed. The bank has already made some concessions to appease its Belgian employees, *customers, and government. Few people lost their jobs as a result of the merger, and BNP opened four global competence centers in Brussels to show that the bank wants to create a stronger presence on the national and global level.*

These kinds of situations are difficult to go through, but there is a change-management process. First there is denial, then asking, "Why us, after all we've accomplished?" But eventually you digest what's happened.

In my experience, there are different types of groups and efforts to be done around employee engagement after a merger:

→ *Employees who are part of the integration project usually don't resist much and embrace the new reality fast. If put on the front line, they tend to become great ambassadors.*

→ *Employees who are very positively impacted, that is, those who take a leadership position in the new organization or find a better job remain engaged but are usually very few.*

→ *Employees who are positively impacted, that is, those who are looking for a change and take the opportunity of the merger to take a redundancy package remain engaged but are also few.*

→ *Employees who are negatively impacted, those that lose power, whose position loses weight in the organization, or who have to report to someone else are usually the majority of the taken-over organization. Those employees are heavily impacted and need lots of effort to reengage. I have experienced two approaches: Either you invest heavily in helping them go through the transition (via the Kubler-Ross change management curve), or you do nothing and expect them (that is, force them) to embrace the new reality. The latter tends to work for a while, although most of the employees will never feel as engaged as in the past ("our company was much better" syndrome).*

So although it requires more effort and patience, in the long term, investing in proper change management is the best for full integration.

Business software maker SAP launched its Social Sabbatical in a recent year to help entrepreneurs and small businesses compete in emerging markets. They also gave employees the chance to work on international teams, and gave them the training needed to succeed. To help develop businesses and infrastructure for poor communities around the world, employees go on a paid four-week sabbatical.

At PwC, a $36 billion professional services firm, employees have countless opportunities for growth, travel, and leadership experiences. PwC hired more than 5,500 new college grads in the past year and started a student loan pay-down benefit of up to $1,200 a year per employee.

Sales professionals at Novartis Pharmaceuticals highly value their compensation and the company's level of commitment to the community. Known for developing and providing free drugs to people who cannot afford to pay, Novartis regularly informs its employees about their contributions to reinforce the notion that the company does what it says it will do.

Over a nine-year period, Campbell's Soup dramatically increased employee engagement. At the beginning of the period, 62 percent of employees were disengaged. CEO Douglas Conant demonstrated his commitment to improving employee engagement by advocating for a number of changes. He removed the barbed-wire fencing around corporate headquarters. He initiated communication workshops to help managers improve relationships with their direct reports. He started having people evaluate their managers, and poorly performing managers were replaced by people within the company. He also wrote personal thank-you notes to high-achieving employees. At the end of the period, 68 percent of employees were actively engaged. Company earnings increased up to 4 percent per year.

Zappos has a corporate goal of creating fun and weirdness at work. At their annual Bald and Blue Day, employees raise money for charities by shaving their heads or dying their hair blue.

Taj Hotels, part of Indian Hotels Company, hired prospective front-line staff from small cities and towns, believing that the "people coming from these areas appreciated traditional values such as respect for elders, honesty, loyalty, and empathy," according to management papers. They recruited directly from high schools and conducted tests to judge candidates' integrity, consistency, ability to work under pressure, and go beyond the call of duty.

Alibaba founder and CEO Jack Ma's love of martial arts is evident everywhere in the work culture. The company values are known as Six Vein Spirit Sword. Each vein represents a company value—customer first, teamwork, embrace change, integrity, passion, and commitment. Employee performance ratings are partly based on how well employees demonstrate the values. Workers select a martial arts nickname for themselves, which are only used in meetings, emails or performance reviews. Vice president of global initiatives Bryan Wong says, "We use the nicknames, and the broader martial arts motif to inspire staff to think of themselves as outsiders fighting for a cause."

Analytics company Hotjar has fifty employees, all of whom work remotely across sixteen countries. It offers employees two company retreats a year, €4,000 to set up a home office, free Fitbit, and a €2,000 budget for vacation.

SmithCorp, an education recruitment company in Bristol, England, has always tied incentives to performance. The company's 140 employees compete for annual all-expenses-paid holidays. They are also eligible to receive free lunches and even a Rolex watch if they make certain numbers. Free breakfast is provided daily in the newly added "hub." Chief development officer James Hodkinson says, "We're growing up as a business. Thirty or forty years ago, employers weren't doing a lot of these things, but I think there's an expectation from potential employees that you're doing a bit more."

> What makes employees come to work is a sense of pride, recognition, and achievement. Workers committed to their jobs and recognized for their work will work whatever hours it takes to get the job done.
>
> —THOMAS KELLEY, FORMER CHAIRMAN OF THE BOARD, SOCIETY FOR HUMAN RESOURCE MANAGEMENT

To ensure their new dogs become acclimated at home, craft beer company Brewdog in Scotland gives employees a paid week off from work.

ZPG, an Internet and real estate company based in London, England, offers interest-free loans for home improvements and weddings.

FEATURED COMPANIES

B&Q,
p. 98
Eastleigh, United Kingdom
Home improvement retailer

Bain & Company,
p. 211
Boston, MA
Management consulting

Balancing Professionals,
p. 233
Cary, NC
Staffing firm

Baskerville-Donovan,
p. 94
Pensacola, FL.
Engineering firm

BaubleBar,
p. 138
New York City, NY
Jewelry retailer

Baxter International,
p. 76
Deerfield, IL
Health-care provider

Bay Area Rapid Transit,
p. 62
St. Oakland, CA
Public transportation

Baylor Scott & White Health,
p. 186
Temple, TX
Health-care system

Beaverbrooks the Jewellers Ltd.,
p. 80, 202
Lytham St. Annes, UK
Fine jewelers

Belatrix,
p. 64
Latin America
Software development services

Benchmark Community Bank,
p. 38
Kenbridge, VA
Financial services

Berryhill Baja Grill,
p. 155
Houston, TX
Mexican restaurant chain

Beryl Corporation,
p. 163
Dallas, TX
Health care

Best Buy,
p. 66, 96, 97, 135, 151, 236
Richfield, MN
Consumer electronics retailer

Betabrand,
p. 229
San Francisco, CA
Clothing retailer

Beth Israel Deaconess Medical Center,
p. 168, 199
Boston, MA
Health care

Black & Veatch,
p. 211
Overland Park, KS
Engineering and construction

Bloomingdale's,
p. 66
New York City, NY
Department store chain

Cargill Inc.,
p. 157
Wayzata, MN
Provider of food, agriculture, financial, and industrial products.

Casper,
p. 239
New York City, NY
Mattress brand

Champion Solutions Group,
p. 90
Boca Raton, FL
Advertising agency

Chegg,
p. 239
Santa Clara, CA
Textbook rentals

Chevron,
p. 62
San Ramon, CA
Multinational energy corporation

Chick-fil-A,
p. 246
Atlanta, GA.
Fast-food restaurant chain

Children's Home Society,
p. 94
Chicago, IL
Social and welfare service provider

Chrysler,
p. 160
Auburn Hills, MI
Automobile manufacturer

Cidera Therapeutics,
p. 204
San Diego, CA
Pharmaceuticals

Cigna Group,
p. 163
Hartford, CT
Insurance company

Circle,
p. 178
Panhandle, TX
Social enterprise delivering health care

Cisco Systems,
p. 48, 67, 80, 168, 198, 209
San Jose, CA
Computer network hardware manufacturer

City of Dallas,
p. 33
Dallas, TX
City government

Citigroup Inc.,
p. 77, 122, 231
New York City, NY
Investment banking and financial services corporation

Coca-Cola Bottling Company,
p. 46, 144, 242
Charlotte, NC
Bottling and distribution

CoCaLo Inc.,
p. 97
Costa Mesa, CA
Baby bedding and accessory manufacturer

Coinbase,
p. 147, 209
San Francisco, CA
Digital coin exchange

Colin Service Systems,
p. 44
Springfield, VA
Faculty service company

Columbus Fair Auto Auction,
p. 158
Columbus, OH
Automobile dealer

Continental Airlines,
p. 192
Houston, TX
Airline carrier

Convercent,
p. 209
Denver, CO
Compliance software

Coors,
p. 200
Golden, CO
Brewing company

Core Creative,
p. 34-35
Milwaukee, WI
Full-service advertising
and branding agency

Costco,
p. 140
Issaquah, WA
Membership-only
warehouse clubs

Covario Inc.,
p. 196
San Diego, CA
Interactive market-
ing analytics software
signer

CRC Health Group,
p. 215
Cupertino, CA
Drug addiction treat-
ment center

Credit Karma,
p. 64
San Francisco, CA
Personal finance
company

Crescendo Strategies,
p. 95, 109, 208
Jeffersonville, IN
Management
consulting

CRST International Trucking,
p. 63
Warrenton, NC
Trucking company

Cummins,
p. 249
Columbus, IN
Engine designer, manu-
facturer, and distributor

CUNA Mutual Group,
p. 247
Madison, WI
Insurance company

Cushman & Wakefield,
p. 50, 233
Portugal, NY
Global real estate firm

Cushman Wakefield,
p. 191
Portugal, Spain
Global real estate firm

CustomInk,
p. 228-229
Fairfax, VA
Online retailer

D&D Interior & Fashion House,
p. 74
Charlotte, NC
Interior design

Da Vita,
p. 197
Segundo, CA
Dialysis service provider

Dwyer Engineering,
p. 150
Leesburg, VA
Engineering and
construction

Dyson,
p. 100, 187
Wiltshire, England
Designer and manu-
facturer of household
appliances

**E.I. du Pont de
Nemours & Company,**
p. 134
Belle, WV
Chemical manufacturer

**East Boston Savings
Bank,**
p. 98
Peabody, MA
Bank

Edward Jones,
p. 142
St. Louis, MO
Financial advisory firm

Eli Lilly & Company,
p. 70
Indianapolis, IN
Pharmaceuticals

**Employee Engagement
Group**
p. 236
Woburn, MA

Entergy,
p. 244
New Orleans, LA
Energy company

Epson,
p. 71
Nagano, Japan.
Electronics

**EY (formerly Ernst &
Young),**
p. 163
New York City, NY
Multinational profes-
sional services firm

**ENSR International
Corporation,**
p. 166
Chelmsford, MA
Environmental
consultant

EXL Service,
p. 216
New York City, NY
Operations manage-
ment and analytics

**Expand Executive
Search,**
p. 44
New York City, NY
Recruiting firm

Facebook,
p. 44, 196, 216, 221
Menlo Park, CA
Social networking
platform

**Fairmont Hotels &
Resorts,**
p. 46
Ontario, Canada
Luxury resort chain

**Farm Bureau Financial
Services,**
p. 116
Des Moines, IA
Life insurance and
financial assistance

FedEx,
p. 106
Memphis, TN
Delivery services

Ferrari S.p.A,
p. 77, 198, 233
Maranello, Italy
Automobile
manufacturer

Fifth Third Bank,
p. 230
Cincinnati, OH.
Bank

First Chester County Corporation,
p. 156, 161
West Chester, PA
Retail and commercial
banking services

First National Bank,
p. 156, 161
West Chester, PA
Financial services

FKP Architects, *p. 79*
Houston, TX
Architecture firm

Fleishman-Hillard,
p. 197
St. Louis, MO
Public relations firm

Flight Centre UK,
p. 88, 138
Malden, UK
Travel agency

Ford Motor Company,
p. 166
Dearborn, MI
Automobile manufac-
turer and distributor

Fortis,
p. 250-252
Grenchen, Switzerland
Watch manufacturer

Full Beaker Inc.,
p. 61, 191
Bellevue, WA
SEO software services

Full Contact,
p. 228
Denver, CO
Software

FuzePlay, *p. 243*
Salt Lake City, UT.
Hackable toy designer
and manufacturer

Gallup Organization,
p. 16, 17, 19, 123
Chicago, IL
Marketing research

Gateway Health,
p. 93, 206
Pittsburgh, PA
Health-plan
management

GE Appliances,
p. 236
Louisville, KY
Appliance company

Genentech,
p. 139
San Francisco, CA
Biotechnology

General Electric Corporation,
p. 72
Fairfield, CT
Electrical contractor

General Electric,
p. 62, 72, 140, 146, 162
Boston, MA
Corporate
conglomerate

General Mills,
p. 72
Minneapolis, MN
Food manufacturer

General Motors,
p. 161-162
Detroit, MI
Automobile
manufacturer

Gensler,
p. 141, 242
San Francisco, CA
Design and architectur-
al firm

Georgetown University Hospitals,
p. 139
Washington, DC
Health care

Giordano International,
p. 236
Hong Kong, China
Clothing retailer

Glossier,
p. 166
New York City, NY
Skin care company

Google,
p. 42, 86, 136, 180, 191, 216, 235
Mountain View, CA
Technology company

Great Harvest Bread Company,
p. 187
Temecula, CA
Baked goods franchise

Growth Works,
p. 45
Vancouver, British Columbia
Early stage technology development

Gucci,
p. 134
Milan, Italy
World-class luxury products

Hadady Corporation,
p. 225
Dyer, IN
Precision manufacturing and distribution

Harmon International Industries Inc.,
p. 75
Stamford, CT
Designs connected products for enterprises worldwide

Hartford Healthcare,
p. 36
Hartford, CT
Health-care services

Harvard Business Publishing,
p. 84
Boston, MA
Business publications

Harvard Vanguard Medical Associates,
p. 186
Boston, MA
Medical practice

Hausmann-Johnson Insurance,
p. 170-171
Madison, WI
Insurance company

Health IQ,
p. 154
Mountain View, CA
Life insurance startup

Hearthstone,
p. 128
Seattle, WA
Retirement home facility

Henry Ford Health System,
p. 98
Detroit, MI
Health-care provider

Herbert Construction Company,
p. 39, 147, 175
Metro Atlanta, GA
Construction services

SAP,
p. 236, 254
Walldorf, Germany
Software solutions

SAS Institute,
p. 92, 163, 167, 174,
230, 237, 240, 245,
246,
Cary, NC
Software manufacturer

Saudi Telecom,
p. 87
Riyadh, Saudi Arabia
Telecommunications

Schlumberger,
p. 199
Houston, TX
Oil field services

Schoenen Torfs,
p. 177
Sint-Niklaas, Belgium
Shoe retailer

Screwfix,
p. 176
Yeovil, England
Home improvement
retailer

Scripps Health,
p. 222
San Diego, CA
Health-care provider

**Self Regional
Healthcare**,
p. 57, 95
Greenwood, SC
Health-care provider

SEO,
p. 61, 191
Lewes, DE
Internet marketing

Serco,
p. 182
Hook, England
Service company

SHI International,
p. 204
Somerset, NJ
Distributor and reseller
of information tech-
nology products and
services

Siemens,
p. 62
Berlin, Germany
Engineering and elec-
tronics conglomerate

Six Flags,
p. 203
Eastchester, NY
Amusement park

Skullcandy,
p. 243
Park City, UT
Audio products
manufacturer

Slack Technologies,
p. 212, 236
Vancouver, Canada
Software company

Slice,
p. 138-139
New York City, NY
Marketplace for pizza
ordering

Small Girls PR,
p. 44
New York City, NY
Public relations firm

Smith & Hawken,
p. 160
Novato, CA
Garden lifestyle brand

Valve,
p. 134, 140
Bellevue, WA
Video game developer and digital distribution

Villa Healthcare,
p. 148
Skokie, IL
Health-care center

Visa,
p. 236
Foster City, CA
Financial services

Visionary Consulting,
p. 110
Shanghai, China
Strategic planning services

Visual Marketing Systems Inc.,
p. 107
Twinsburg, OH
Graphic design

W.L. Gore & Associates,
p. 200
Newark, DE
Fabric manufacturer

Walmart,
p. 65, 66, 138, 169, 216
Bentonville, AR
Major retailer

Wegmans,
p. 87, 166
Rochester, NY
Supermarket chain

WellStar Health System,
p. 242
Marietta, GA
Health-care services

Wendy's International,
p. 70
Dublin, OH
Fast-food restaurant chain

West Marine,
p. 239
Watsonville, CA
Boating supply retailer

WeWork,
p. 240
New York, NY
Shared workspaces and related services for entrepreneurs

Whole Foods,
p. 87
Austin, TX
Food company

Wild Creation,
p. 40
Arlington, TX
Business service provider

Winegardner & Hammons Inc.,
p. 85
Cincinnati, OH
Hotel management firm

ACKNOWLEDGEMENTS

A book like this is harder than it looks to pull together, and the journey of this particular book spanned multiple iterations over a dozen years.

I want to thank researchers who helped me on this project including Nick Swisher, Austin Becker, Peter Economy, Rebecca Taff, and Jeanie Casison, as well as the hundreds of people that submitted examples and stories for this book. My good friend and colleague of over thirty years, Mario Tamayo, served as project manager extraordinaire in helping to pull all elements of this book together in a timely, organized manner. Ashlyn Withers constructed the index of featured companies in the book with help from Zach Osborne.

A big thanks to my friend and colleague Marshall Goldsmith for writing the book's foreword, as well as his insights and hours of discussion with me on the topic of employee engagement; likewise, Bob Kelleher, founder of The Engagement Group (*www.employeeengagement.com*) and author of numerous books on the topic, including *Louder than Words: 10 Practical Employee Engagement Steps that Drive Results,* and *I-Engage: Your Personal Engagement Roadmap*; and special thanks to Kevin Sheridan (*www.kevinsheridanllc.com*), noted authority on employee engagement and author of *Building a Magnetic Culture* and *The Virtual Manager* for use of his research on employee engagement he conducted while CEO of HR Solutions, as well as several examples from his books and blog.

Plus all the dedicated folks at Career Press/Red Wheel/Weiser, including Michael Pye, the senior acquisitions editor who won the bidding war for this book due to his vision and enthusiasm to publish it.

ABOUT THE AUTHOR

D r. Bob Nelson is considered a leading authority on employee recognition, motivation, and engagement. He is president of Nelson Motivation, a management training and consulting company that specializes in helping organizations improve their management practices, programs, and systems. He serves as an executive strategist for human resource issues, has worked with 80 percent of the Fortune 500, and has been named a Top Thought Leader by the Best Practice Institute and a Global 100 Employee Engagement Influencer. He previously worked closely with Dr. Ken Blanchard, *"The One Minute Manager"* for ten years and currently serves as a personal coach for Dr. Marshall Goldsmith, the world's number-one-ranked executive coach.

Dr. Bob has sold five million books on management and employee motivation, including *1,501 Ways to Reward Employees*, *Recognizing & Engaging Employees for Dummies*, *The 1,001 Rewards & Recognition Fieldbook*, *1,001 Ways to Energize Employees*, *The Management Bible*, and *Ubuntu!* among others. His books have been translated into thirty-seven languages. He has presented on six continents and has appeared extensively in the national and international media including CBS's 60 Minutes, CNN, MSNBC, CNBC, PBS, National Public Radio, as well as in *the New York Times, the Wall Street Journal, the Washington Post, the Chicago Tribune, Fortune, BusinessWeek,* and *Inc.* magazines to discuss how to best motivate today's employees. *Corporate Meetings & Incentives* dubbed him "The Guru of Thank You"; *Workforce Management* called him "The King of Rewards."

Dr. Bob holds a BA in psychology and communications from Macalester College (St. Paul, Minnesota), received an MBA in organizational behavior from UC Berkeley, and earned his PhD in management education with the late, great Dr. Peter Drucker, "The Father of Modern Management," at the Drucker Graduate Management School of Claremont Graduate University in Los Angeles; his doctoral dissertation was entitled "Factors that Encourage or Inhibit the Use of Employee Recognition by US Managers."

Dr. Bob is available to consult with your organization on how to create a better recognition and engagement culture (including finding the best vendor partner for your needs) or to present for your company, conference, or association on topics related to his books and research. You can reach him directly at Nelson Motivation (*www.drbobnelson.com*), at (858) 673-0690, via email at bob@drbobnelson.com, or via LinkedIn at *www.linkedin.com/in/drbobnelson*.

NOTES

NOTES